D1490622

SCHIRMER BOOKS
THEATRE
MANUALS

STAGE DESIGN AND PROPERTIES

Michael Holt

Series editor: David Mayer

SCHIRMER BOOKS

For Els, Harry and David.

Acknowledgements
The author and the publisher gratefully acknowledge the
help and assistance of the students and staff at the Royal
Academy of Dramatic Art, London for their participation
in the photographs taken by Michael Prior.

Photographs: Carol Baugh pp.24–25, 105; Michael Prior
pp. 39, 65, 67, 69, 74, 82–83, 84–85, 100–101, 112, 114, 116,
117, 118–119, 120.

Illustrations: Jones, Sewell and Associates pp.18–19, 20,
23, 33, 34, 35, 43, 44–45, 61, 63, 71, 72–73, 76–77, 78–79,
80–81, 86–87, 88–89, 90–91, 93, 95, 96–97, 98–99, 108,
110–111, 112–113, 114–115, 116–117, 118–119, 120; Miller, Craig
and Cocking pp. 9, 10–11, 12, 13, 26–27, 41, 68, 70.

First American edition published in 1989 by
Schirmer Books

A Division of Macmillan, Inc.

Copyright © 1988 by Phaidon Press Limited,
Oxford 1988

Schirmer Books
A Division of Macmillan, Inc.
866 Third Avenue, New York, N. Y. 10022

First published in Great Britain by
Phaidon Press Limited, Oxford

Library of Congress Catalog Card Number: 88-18167

Printed and bound in Singapore under co-ordination by
C S Graphics Pte Ltd

printing number
1 2 3 4 5 6 7 8 9 10

**Library of Congress Cataloging-in-Publication
Data**

Holt, Michael.
  Stage design and properties

  Bibliography: p.
  Includes index
  1. Theaters – Stage-setting and scenery.
2. Stage props.   3. Set designers.   I. Title.
PN2091.S8H65 1989   792'.025–025   88-15789
ISBN 0-02-871343-5

ISBN 0-02-871341-9 (set)

Designed by Miller, Craig and Cocking, Woodstock

Contents

INTRODUCTION

Work in the theatre is always undertaken with a future performance in mind, but two artistic facts of life affect this work. One is that no one, no matter how naturally talented and accomplished, can invariably count on inspiration to solve a problem. The other fact is that time is the most precious of all theatrical commodities. The date of a first performance is an unalterable deadline, and that deadline, in turn, determines a whole sequence of earlier deadlines which must be met within the resources, not always ideal, that are available to the theatrical team.

These facts have been our starting-point in devising this series. Inspiration may be rare, but creativity, we suggest, can be supplemented by technique. Effective organization coupled with careful forward-planning can result in impressive productions. Experience has shown that good preparation will actually free the creative imagination and give it room to flourish.

This series has been designed to meet the needs of those working in the non-professional theatre, that is students and undergraduates, school teachers, and members of amateur dramatic and operatic societies. This is not an indication of the standards of the performances to be achieved; some amateur productions are quite outstanding. In fact some of the differences between the amateur and the professional are in the amateurs' favour: amateur groups can often call upon enormous resources for behind-the-scenes labour and the large casts that are so often out of reach of most professional companies. But non-professionals are more likely to be limited by the amount of time, money, space and materials available. We recognize that you will be working with some or all of these advantages and restrictions, and we offer ways of looking at problems which will stimulate the imagination and produce solutions. The answers will then be yours, not ours.

Putting on a play is essentially teamwork, teamwork which depends upon the creativity of administrators and craftsmen, performers, directing staff and stage crews. The team can best thrive when responsibilities are shared and lines of communiciation are always open, direct and cordial. In recognition of these needs we have linked the books by planning charts and repeating themes looked at from different angles in order to emphasize that the best results are always achieved when skills are pooled.

Dozens of performances and hours of discussion lie behind these texts, and while we cannot claim to have covered every eventuality, we are confident that the approach outlined in the following pages will lead to productions that are successful, imaginative, and, above all, enjoyable for you, your colleagues, and your audiences.

David Mayer

Safety

Attention to safety is vitally important when you are putting on any production. When there is a procedure in this book where special care must be taken a safety flash ⚡ *has been inserted in the margin.*

CHAPTER I

THE ROLE OF THE DESIGNER

The kind and amount of design work you will do on a production will depend on the script you have, the size and nature of your theatre company and its budget. However you can get an idea of your function and responsibilities by considering the simple question:

WHY A DESIGNER?

As designer you provide an educated eye. You should be well informed about the historical period of the play and know precisely how things should look. You should also be sensitive to every visual effect, able to recognize exactly what atmosphere or mood is contributed by a colour, a shape, a light or a shadow. You must be both informed and visually responsive.

The director guides creativity within rehearsals. The designer has a similar function with the technical craftsmen. You become a focus for their work, a reference point for their imaginative contributions. You must be able to communicate clearly and sympathetically with the whole production team.

You cannot work beside every individual craftsman or technician, but you can impart visual information in the form of scale models, prop drawings, technical diagrams, photographs and written description. You need a fertile imagination and a capacity to solve technical problems inventively. Throughout production you will be called on to provide visually appropriate solutions to difficulties with sets or props as well as inventing visual effects. Most problems will have been anticipated in the planning stages but unforeseen ones will need confronting during the building period.

WHAT MAKES A GOOD DESIGNER?

The designer is a combined draughtsman and model maker, technician, psychologist and team leader who can inspire trust and imaginative responses in others.

Mounting a theatrical production is a group activity; total cooperation is essential. The team will contain many talents, and part of your job is to recognize and capitalize on them. You must communicate ideas clearly to the appropriate people – director, stage manager, technical director, craftsmen, actors – while understanding *their* problems and producing design solutions to them.

GOOD SET DESIGN

There are three questions to ask about any set design, and you should constantly ask them as you prepare your own:

Does it help the actor?
visual splendour that gets in the way is bad design. Any weakening of an actor's effectiveness – by a poorly placed door, a prop of inconvenient size, a badly angled window – is to be deplored. No actor should have to combat the visual effects. The set designer must fuse actor and setting together *for the benefit of the action*. If they seem separate and the actor uncomfortable, the designer has failed.

Does it add atmosphere, mood, style?
A good set immediately presents the characters within a detailed frame.
Historical detail tells us where and when the play is set – it establishes the country and the period.
Colours and shapes add mood – warm or cool, sinister or jovial.
Texture – lush or rough-hewn surfaces – conveys the social milieu.
The overall pictorial style communicates the play's genre – comic, tragic, romantic.
You will learn to evaluate a setting by the amount of factual and psychological information it contains.

HAS THE INTENTION BEEN REALIZED?

There are several reasons why it may not have been – lack of money, lack of time, lack of planning, lack of facilities.
Every designer, not only the amateur, faces these limitations. All of them can be got round with forethought, and by emphasizing planning. A good designer assesses his resources and works within them. No lack of resource need be overwhelming. Reduced to a mere table and a chair, you can get them exactly right and still produce a good design in the terms suggested here.

THE PRODUCTION DIARY

Mounting a production is a complex process stretching over many weeks and involving a lot of people, often working in different places. How many people and places, and how much time is spent on the production will vary with each company, so one cannot offer a universal blueprint for a production diary. The one given here will help. It shows what processes have to be assigned and completed. The order suggested is the most practical, but individual circumstances may call for some adaptation.
You will be primarily interested in the designer's line but you should make cross-references to other people's diaries to see the consequences for you of decisions they must take. Here again, communication between all parties is essential throughout the period covered by the diary.

THE TECHNICAL DIRECTOR

In many companies the technical directors or production managers act as general supervisors for all the technicians involved. They take care of budget supervision, contracting and production process planning. If your company does not have anyone in this role the responsibilities will have to be undertaken by several people. Be sure to discuss the sharing of these functions before you start and make certain that everyone involved is clear about those duties allocated to them.

PRE-PRODUCTION

Start this period in concept discussions with the director. Meet as often as you can and thoroughly analyse any design proposals. As a result of these talks you will produce your set model, technical drawings (line drawings) and other preliminary art work. Eventually, having agreed on design details, you can meet with the other production people. This is also the time for budget discussions, for a technical team to be assembled and for the anticipation of as many problems as possible. Be sure to give ample time to this preparation process. Discuss carefully the realizing of your designs with your lighting designer, technical director and stage manager. Try to eliminate as many problems as possible at this stage. The reward will be more time to concentrate on the production.

Pre-production Period

Function	Pre-rehearsal Period
Administrator	Check play available for performance. Check score available for performance. Negotiate royalty payments. Check venue available. Pre-production discussions with Director and Designers. Check licensing and permission, especially firearms. Check credit card registration. Gather programme material. Plan publicity. Announce auditions. Determine budget.
Director	Pre-production discussions. Conduct auditions – with choreographer and Musical Director. Announce casting. Announce and initiate rehearsal schedules.
Production Manager/ Technical Director	Pre-production budget meeting with Administration. Design meeting with Director, Designer and Stage Manager. Appoint Stage Manager and technical staff.
Stage Management	Attend design meeting and run auditions. Prepare prompt copy and provisional lists. Research with designer. Gather rehearsal props, furniture and set. Find a rehearsal space.
Scenic Design and Construction	Pre-production discussions. Model making: technical and working. Prepare drawings. Prepare prop drawings. Get Director's approval. Prepare castings and planning.
Lighting	Pre-production discussions. Read and re-read text. Research & Planning costume and scene.
Sound	Pre-production discussions. Read and re-read text. Prepare a selection of provisional tapes. Get Director's approval.
Music	Check availability of scores. Organize a rehearsal pianist. Audition singers. Agree rehearsal schedule with Director. Gather orchestra.
Choreography Fights	Check rehearsal space. Organize rehearsal pianist. Audition dancers. Agree rehearsal schedule with Director.
Costume Design and Construction	Pre-production discussions. Costume research and drawing. Working drawings for wigs/hats/shoes. Fabric sampling. Costing and planning.

Function	Week 6	Week 5	Week 4	Week 3
Administration	Gather programme material. Display publicity material. Open booking if necessary.	Start press stories. Monitor publicity. Monitor bookings. Contact with rehearsals.	Recruit FOH staff if required. Invite critics.	Direct sell.
Director	Attend production meeting. ■ Discussions ■ Script cuts ■ Note running time.	Blocking rehearsal.	Business rehearsals. Rehearsal props introduced. Attend meetings. Listen to sound tape. Lighting meeting	Singers and dancers integrated. Reblocking. ■ Pianist present. Orchestral rehearsal
Production Manager	Costing meetings with set, prop and costume makers. Production meeting. Problem solving and budget decisions.	Coordinating technical departments and budget control.		Progress meeting. Arrange for equipment ■ Liaison with venue.
Stage Management	Mark out and prepare rehearsal space. Note script changes. Attend production and props meetings.	Run rehearsal Prop, furniture and dressings search and making. Liaison with all departments.		Attend progress meeting Arrange sound and lighti meetings for director
Scenic design and construction	Meetings and planning with technical director. ■ Attend read through Call for actors, staff and workshop. Scenic construction and propmaking.	Liaison with SM and workshop. ■ Buy soft furnishings.	■ Choose hire furniture and scene painting.	Drawings for new props. Alterations as necessary.
Costume design and construction make up	Attend first rehearsal.	Artwork and photography for projection. ■ Construction special lighting affects.	Preliminary fittings.	
Lighting	Attend production meeting. Keep in contact rehearsals – SM/Director/Designer. Liaison with Director and Designer		■ Check stock.	Attend rehearsal and run through.
Sound	Attend production meeting. Basic provisional tape in rehearsal.	Research and planning. ■ Check stock and buy in tapes, effects records, etc. Meeting with director.	Prepare effects tapes. Sound meetings with director.	Record special effects. Record hire effects with actors. ■ Design sound rig. ■ Hire equipment.
Music	Singing rehearsals. Music rehearsals.			Singers join main rehears
Choreography and fights	Dancing rehearsals. Fight rehearsals.		Hire weapons with SM.	Fights choreographed. Dancers join main rehea

Week 2	Day 7	Day 6	Day 5	Day 4	Day 3	Day 2	Day 1
vite press to otocall.	Check Box. Engage FOH staff. ■ Ushers. ■ Sales. ■ Box Office.	Train FOH staff. Arrange FOH displays. Print programmes.				Photo call.	
ish rehearsal. Fights in rehearsal. eet to discuss lighting. eet with sound dept, to eck final FX.	Introduce performance props.		Run through	Attend lighting and sound plotting sessions.	Attend technical rehearsal and give notes.	Photo call, dress rehearsal give notes.	Final dress rehearsal and gives notes.
ark up production hedule. Arrange transport d staff for the get in/fit up d show staff.	Supervise get in and fit up as per production schedule	Continue fit up as per schedule (+ LX main rig).	Continue as per schedule. Possible fire inspection	Supervise schedule. (LX and sound plotting sessions).	Attend technical rehearsal.	Supervise technical work on stage. Attend dress rehearsal.	Supervise technical work on stage. Attend final dress rehearsal.
rrange lighting designer to e an early run through. rector to listen to sound pe. Prepare setting lists d cue sheets.	Run rehearsals. Team attend run through. Finalize setting lists, cue sheets	Help fit up paint etc. Find props adjustments.	Team help more out of rehearsal rooms to venue.	Dress the set Set the props. Attend LX and sound plotting sessions.	Possible scene change rehearsal. Run technical rehearsal.	Run Dress rehearsal. Attend Director's note session.	Run final dress rehearsal.
op meetings to check all ops. tend Lighting Discussion.	Fit up and painting as per production.	Continue fit up and painting as per production schedule.	Fit up and paint end texture as per schedule.	Attend lighting session and LX plotting. Dress the set.	Attend technical rehearsal.	Attend photo call. Attend dress rehearsal.	Technical work as necessary. Attend dress rehearsal.
	Check costumes, Check wigs arrived.	Get in for costumes. Costumes to dressing rooms.	Attend run through.	Attend run through Check make up.	Attend technical rehearsal. Check make up under lights.		
	Finalize copy lighting design. Preliminary rigging. Hired equipment arrives.	Lighting rigging.	Focusing of lighting.	Lighting session plotting.	Technical rehearsal.	Dress rehearsal. Attend notes sessions. Technical work on stage.	Final dress rehearsal. Technical work on stage.
eparation of final tapes. Rehearse live sound xing – mini-tech. rector to hear tape.	Hired equipment arrives. Mini sound tech with orchestra.	Sound rigging.	Attend run through.	Sound plotting rework tapes.	Technical rehearsal. Rework tapes.	Dress rehearsal. Rework tapes. Attend notes session.	Final dress rehearsal. Attend notes session.
usicians rehearse with und reinforcement if cessary.				Rehearsal for orchestra and cast.	Technical rehearsal, piano only.	Dress rehearsal with orchestra.	
ghts join main rehearsal.		Choreographer present as needed.					

The Run and Post Production

Function	The Run	Post Production
Administrator	Show reports to Director. FOH staff checks. Monitor sales. Liaise with Stage Manager.	File prompt script and production paperwork. Collect scripts. Pay accounts.
Director	Note running times. Director's notes to cast. Warnings and encouragement before performance. Keep contact with SM for problems.	File director's script. Compile report on production and contact list for cast or production team.
Production Manager	Work on budget accounts with Administration. Check orchestra pit.	Arrange transport and staff for get-out. Supervise get-out and storage of any stock set. Supervise returns of hired/borrowed equipment. Final work on accounts with Administration return scores.
Stage Management	Run shows as per prompt script, running lists, etc. Check set, props, furniture settings. Supervise understudy rehearsals. Show reports.	Get out props, dressings and furniture. Supervise return of hired and borrowed items and stock to stores. Assemble prompt script and all lists, plots, etc. for the show and file with Administration.
Scenic Design and Construction		Sort out scenic stock to keep with Production Manager.
Lighting	Check performances crew present. Check equipment pre-performance. Run Show.	Dismantle and store lighting equipment. Return hired equipment. File lighting plot.
Sound	Check performances crew present. Check equipment pre-performance. Run Show.	Dismantle and store sound equipment. Store tapes and catalogue for future. Return hired equipment.
Costume Design		Cleaning and storage of costumes. File costume Bible.

THE TEAM

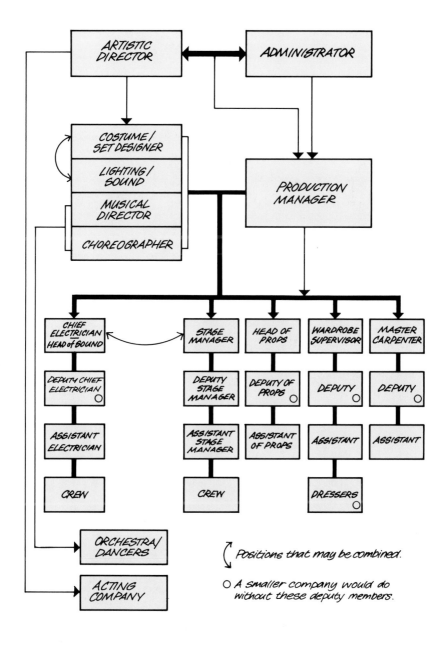

ARTISTIC DIRECTOR ◄──► ADMINISTRATOR

COSTUME / SET DESIGNER
LIGHTING / SOUND
MUSICAL DIRECTOR
CHOREOGRAPHER

PRODUCTION MANAGER

CHIEF ELECTRICIAN HEAD of SOUND
DEPUTY CHIEF ELECTRICIAN ○
ASSISTANT ELECTRICIAN
CREW

STAGE MANAGER
DEPUTY STAGE MANAGER
ASSISTANT STAGE MANAGER
CREW

HEAD OF PROPS
DEPUTY OF PROPS ○
ASSISTANT OF PROPS

WARDROBE SUPERVISOR
DEPUTY ○
ASSISTANT
DRESSERS ○

MASTER CARPENTER
DEPUTY ○
ASSISTANT

ORCHESTRA / DANCERS

ACTING COMPANY

⌐ Positions that may be combined.

○ A smaller company would do without these deputy members.

13

WORKSHOP AND REHEARSAL TIME

Before rehearsals start you will have to present your design to the cast and production team at the preliminary read-through. Be sure to point out restricted access, cramped acting areas or any other parts of your design that may affect presentation.

Check the stage management's mark-out of your ground plan on the rehearsal room floor. Mistakes here can cause great problems later. Establish good communication with stage management so that you will be kept constantly in touch with developments. If you are asked for new designs to meet rehearsal inventions be sure that you understand exactly what is proposed. Though very busy you should try to attend at least some rehearsals to see just how the production is developing. It will give you a clearer idea of any adjustments that you may be asked for.

While rehearsals are under way you will be overseeing the building and painting of the setting and props. The clearer you have been in telling the crafts people what is intended the freer you will be during this period. At some point you will need to visit the theatrical hirers to choose those props not being made specially for the production.

FIT UP (PUT-IN), DRESS REHEARSALS, OPENING

Once the setting is assembled on stage you must be available for any last-minute adjustments or changes that need discussing, and you must attend the lighting sessions. Though the lighting designer will make the major decisions here you will want to see their effects on your work.

You will attend technical and dress rehearsals to see that the set works as you planned and that it really helps the actors in putting the story across.

At the first-night performance you must be as supportive as possible to director, cast, stage management and, of course, publicity department.

Some companies require the designer to help in the post-production period, returning borrowed properties, deciding about storage of scenery and various other matters.

THE DESIGNER'S RESPONSIBILITIES

Your work during the production period will be varied. First you will prepare a model set in response to discussions with the play's director. Then you will provide the workshops with technical plans and prop designs, and stage management with lists of information. You will have to follow the progress of your designs as they are realized, liaising with craftsmen, responding to new ideas from the rehearsal room and choosing materials and hired properties. All this may also be overseen by your technical director, who will have given you a budget that will affect many of your choices. As performance draws near you will attend the get-in (load-in), the lighting of your setting, the technicals and the dress rehearsals.

This is a lot of responsibility, and it can only be discharged effectively if you co-operate closely with the rest of the production team.

YOU AND THE DIRECTOR

Ideally the director/designer relationship should be one in which imaginative ideas are freely exchanged without inhibition. This needs mutual trust and confidence, and explains why many director/designer partnerships have proved so durable.

Of course, directors may use solely their own ideas, imposing their vision on their designers and using them merely as technicians. Work with such a person is very unrewarding; an efficient but pedestrian production is its likely outcome.

It is important that you have confidence in your director, listening, grasping the core of his or her ideas and interpreting them. Make clear your capacity to respond to production ideas in design terms and to initiate visual interpretations of your own. You must both be able to recognize ideas that have insight and potential whoever suggests them.

DESIGNER AND PRODUCTION TEAM

You will have a team of technicians with you in the workshops who are theatre artists in

their own right. Their skill and care will be very obvious in the finished setting. Good working relations with them are essential, and can only be maintained if you show your confidence in them.

Communication is important. You must make clear in drawings and discussions the basic design concept, exactly what the finished design should look like and how each element fits into the production and how it is to be used. At the same time you must recognize the skills and experience of individual carpenters, painters and prop makers, who will often see ways of getting results that have eluded you. Good communications will enable the team to offer suggestions and will involve them more in achieving exactly the required result. Use your craftspeople to generate ideas; evaluate these ideas and, if they seem better than your own, use them. You are the final arbiter on visual decisions, but not the only source of ideas.

PRODUCTION AND COMMUNICATION

All production teams are slightly different. Some are bigger than others. This diagram on page 13 presents an ideal picture. It emphasizes lines of communication because the designer, director, technical director and craftsmen must keep in touch and discuss problems as they arise.

THE FERTILE IMAGINATION

You will continually be asked for new visual effects to put across things that are invented in rehearsal. Be prepared for this by clearly understanding the ideas at the heart of your design concept. Keep in mind the fundamental style, mood or atmosphere and you will be able to respond to any demand. Ask of any new design suggestion, wherever it comes from, 'Does this fit and enhance the core idea?' You will then be open to inventive solutions but careful about inappropriate ones. Editing out bad ideas is as important as having good ones.

A 'TYPICAL' STAGE?

There is no such thing. Every theatre is unique, with its own special features and idiosyncrasies. Our drawing is of a hypothetical example designed to show the elements you need to be familiar with to design a setting. This particular stage has a proscenium arch, since this is still the kind of theatre prevailing in Europe and America.

When introduced to a theatre you should examine conditions in four areas.

■ note the onstage area, its acting space, the amount of forestage and the effect of sightlines
■ what kind of cyclorama is there? Your design may include a sky effect
■ what is the floor of the stage made of? You may need to fix things to it – is it raked, sloping up from downstage to upstage?
■ are there any traps? Find out what the understage contains
■ check the offstage area for its technical facilities
■ how much wing space is there? It will be used for storage and for actors to assemble
■ which side is the prompt corner? If the show is managed from there you will have to design around this fact
■ how will scenery be got on stage from the workshops? The size and position of dock doors is crucial
■ as you walk onstage look up to see what is in the flies – you will want to know the type of flying system, the positions of permanent lighting features and the height the borders are kept at
■ which side is the fly-gallery? Flying will be controlled from here
■ where is the safety curtain? This will affect your ground plan crucially
■ finally look at the auditorium. The relationship of stage to audience is crucial
■ does the seating rise in one slope or are there balconies? The audience's view of the actors is in your hands
■ how far away are the nearest and the furthest seats? That will affect the type of acting needed
■ what kind of lighting is positioned out front? You need to know from where the setting will be lit.

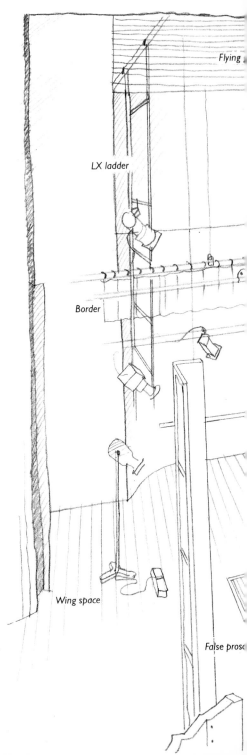

Flying

LX ladder

Border

Wing space

False prosc

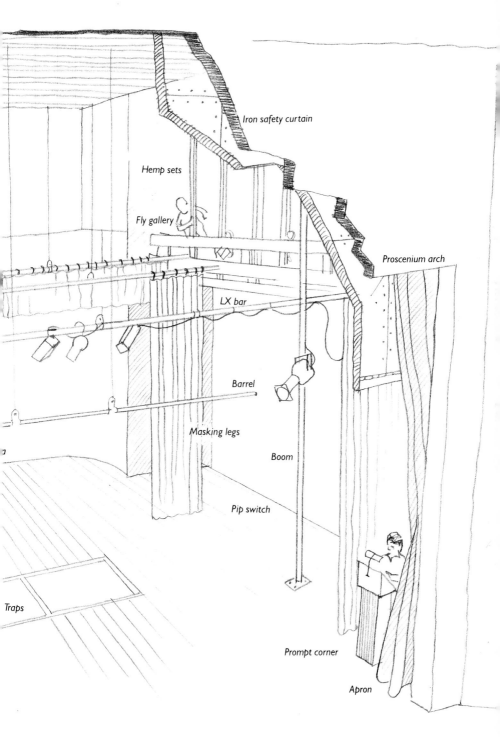

Iron safety curtain

Hemp sets

Fly gallery

LX bar

Barrel

Masking legs

Boom

Pip switch

Traps

Proscenium arch

Prompt corner

Apron

19

The Stage Groundplan: a Diagram.

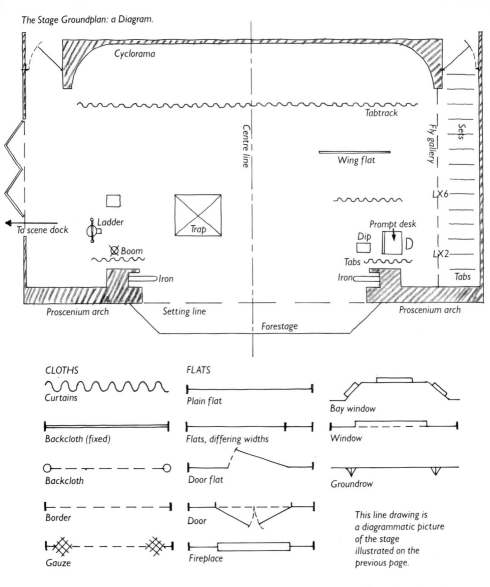

CLOTHS

Curtains

Backcloth (fixed)

Backcloth

Border

Gauze

FLATS

Plain flat

Flats, differing widths

Door flat

Door

Fireplace

Bay window

Window

Groundrow

This line drawing is
a diagrammatic picture
of the stage
illustrated on the
previous page.

THE STAGE GROUND PLAN

A designer must be able to read a ground plan and understand its symbols and descriptions. Every theatre has a printed technical diagram (line diagram) of is layout. It shows the stage as seen from above drawn to scale: usually 1:24 (half-inch = one foot) or 1:25 (one centimetre = twenty-five centimetres). A copy of it is given to anyone planning to design for that particular stage, to show the facilities available.

Look first for the information box in a corner of the drawing. It contains the name of the theatre and the scale of the diagram. You will work to the same scale and your preliminary designing can be done directly on the plan or, preferably, on a tracing of it. If the scale is 1:24 then every half-inch of line that you draw will represent one foot in reality, so you will be able to position things conveniently and judge the proportions of available space.

GROUND PLAN TERMS AND SYMBOLS

Familiarize yourself with these technical terms and symbols so that you can read a theatre ground plan with ease.

ONSTAGE TERMS

PROS: the proscenium arch.

FALSE PROS: a temporary arch for masking inside the architectural proscenium.

TORMENTOR (TEASER): the door or window part of a false proscenium.

FORESTAGE or APRON: two terms for the acting area forward of the proscenium arch.

SETTING LINE: lines marked on the ground plan and used to plan setting positions.

CENTRE LINE: another imaginary line used by designers and stage management.

CYCLORAMA: a plain white or pale blue sky effect, so called because it wraps round the back of the stage. It can be a solid part of the theatre's structure but is often a cloth.

TRAPS: trapdoors provide access to the understage. The flaps can be hinged or on a sliding system.

IRON: this is the safety curtain that crosses the stage on this line.

TABS (ACT-CURTAINS): the theatrical term for the front curtains.

DIPS: electrical points set flush with the stage floor and having hinged metal lids. They are used for practical lighting on stage.

OFFSTAGE TERMS

PROMPT CORNER: the show is sometimes controlled from here. It is usually at stage-left. If placed elsewhere it is called a BASTARD PROMPT.

SCENE DOCK: the storage space.

WINGS: a general term for the areas at the sides of the stage.

WING and LEG: vertical masking. WING is the term used for flats, LEG for an anonymous soft fabric masking. Notice how differently they are drawn on a plan.

BOOM: a vertical metal pole on which lighting is hung.

LADDER: also used for providing added lighting positions.

OVER STAGE TERMS

FLIES: the area above the stage used for the flying system.

GRID: a false ceiling housing the pulleys and ropes for flying, often made of wooden beams or joists.

FLY GALLERY: a balcony at the side of the stage from which the flying system is worked.

SETS: sets of flying lines. The ropes are fixed to BARRELS (BATTENS), metal pipes to which scenery is attached.

L.X: a set marked by this term is fixed as a permanent lighting bar.

TAB TRACK (ACT-CURTAIN TRACK): a metal curtain track crossing the stage and controlled by a line at one end.

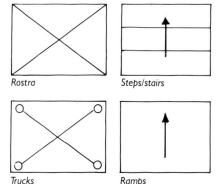

Rostra

Steps/stairs

Trucks

Ramps

THE VARIETY OF THEATRE SHAPES

You may be asked to design for a theatre that has no conventional proscenium-arch stage. A theatre is designed round the demands of its site and the preferences of the commissioning agency, so they are very different, each presenting its own challenge to you as designer.

However, we can class theatres according to the general style of their stage shapes, and though your theatre will have its own features you will recognize it in one of these descriptions. You must be aware of the designing needs for each acting space.

THEATRE IN THE ROUND

If your theatre has the audience seated all round the acting area you cannot build large scenic structures. Without walls to decorate, the design emphasis will be on the floor and furniture. You may be able to extend the design to the entrance gangways, often called 'vomitories', and add flown scenery in a limited form over the stage. But sightlines will be a major problem. People in the front seats must be able to see over the largest object; and they must not feel estranged from the action by sitting behind it.

Treatment of the stage floor will be a big preoccupation. You will need colour and texture that produce exactly the atmospheric quality of the scene. Even though restricted by sightlines you can make it more interesting by breaking the area up into different levels.

Choose precisely and scrutinize closely everything you put on the stage – fabrics, furniture and every property. For example, a framed photograph of a character must be a recognizable likeness, though this is less important on a proscenium stage, where the audience is at a greater distance.

THRUST STAGES

A stage extending out into the audience but attached to a rear acting area tempts the designer to provide a theatre-in-the-round design with a scenic background. To some extent this is almost inevitable. A good thrust stage design marries the two elements together. It is important to try to disguise any division by use of colour, shape and/or texture.

Be aware that your actors will want to get out on to the thrust shape as directly as possible. Facilitate this with a ground plan giving immediate forward access.

Here again properties and stage dressings will need attention to detail, but a thrust stage is a more theatrical space than the naturalistic theatre in the round, and you can use a more exaggerated design style.

TRAVERSE STAGES

Traverse stages are rarer than the others shown here. They allow imaginative scenic images at either end of the acting area but you are really dealing with a theatre in the round again, and focusing on the floor. This time, because the audience is in two blocks directly facing each other, the space between becomes a theatrical bond. The design must use this to create an environment shared by actors and audience. Traverse staging suits this artificial genre better than any other shape.

FLEXIBLE THEATRES

Some theatres are designed to be adapted to several different shapes, allowing a production team to decide which is best for their play. Decisions must be based not only on a production concept, but also on practicalities. A play needing doors for surprise entrances, for instance, is not best served by theatre-in-the-round.

Groundplan for a theatre in the round.

Vomitorium Entrance

Vomitorium Entrance

Stage

Entrance

Groundplan for a thrust stage.

Entrance

Entrance

Stage

Vomitorium Entrance

Steps up

A photograph of the Octagon Theatre, Bolton in England which is a good example of a flexible stage.

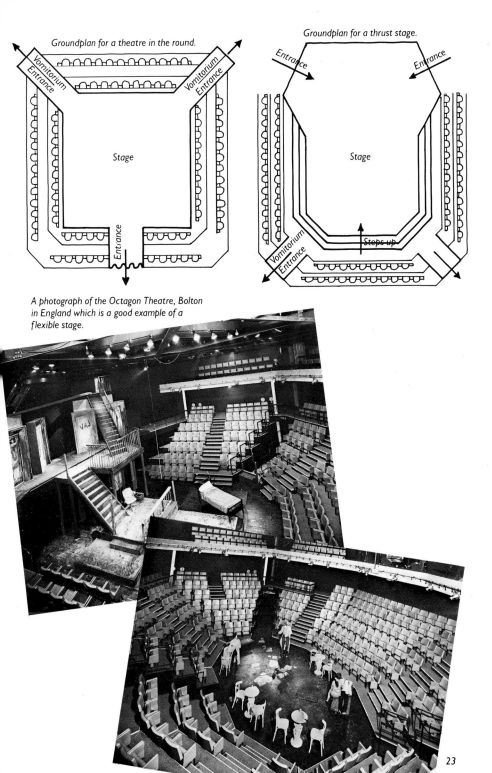

TEMPORARY THEATRES

You may be asked to create a temporary theatre, perhaps on an outdoor site in the grounds of an historic house. Or you might be asked to set up a stage for a graduation ceremony or concert in a non-theatrical hall. Whatever the demand, if you use some imagination and follow a few basic rules you can provide an exciting and unusual venue .

A THEATRE FOR THE AUDIENCE

Audiences will accept an unusual theatre design with little fuss provided that they know how they are expected to behave in it. This applies whether they are asked to gather informally at an impromptu street theatre or complicated temporary seating.

Whatever your temporary theatre you should make obvious the answers to what those attending are likely to ask:

■ how will I get to the theatre? What transport, parking and access will there be? How will I get away if it finishes late?
■ where do I buy my ticket? If it is numbered how do I find my seat? Are all the entrances and gangways clearly marked? Which area is the stage and which the seating? How safe will I be in case of emergency evacuation of the theatre?
■ how will I know when the performance is about to start? Will there be intervals and how will they be signalled as starting and finishing?
■ will I be able to see everything? If not what compensations will the presentation make for this? How uncomfortable will my

seat be? Will I be free to shift around or leave my seat during the show? Where are the toilet facilities in relation to my position?

■ what happens if it rains?

■ will the performance be disturbed by aircraft noise or other sounds?

A THEATRE FOR THE ACTOR

Actors can work in any space, whatever its shape or size, but will always ask those basic performers' questions – how do I get on and off? Can I be seen and heard? The answers are quite complex, and linked to a series of other questions:

■ where do I change into costume? Can I wash, use a mirror, have privacy? Is there a practicewarm-up area? How far are the dressing rooms from the stage? What refreshments will there be for the performers?

■ where is the stage entrance? How far do I travel before I am seen by the whole audience or get to the main acting area? Can I exit by an alternative route to avoid bumping into another performer or to indicate different locations within the play?

■ can I be seen at stage level or do I need a rostrum? Is the audience too close or too far away? How is the division between acting area and auditorium marked?

■ how am I lit? By artificial, theatrical, or natural light? Do I need microphones? Where is the lighting and sound control box, the stage management desk? What kind of power source is available?

■ what happens if it rains?

OUTDOOR VENUES

Study your site with care and take advantage of useful features even if that means having a very unconventional stage shape. Use attractive points and convenient entrances and design your theatre round them. Sometimes the landscape will suggest a natural auditorium position, sometimes a suitable acting area. Pick those most helpful.

Use simple screens to mask entrances and to let actors get from one side of the stage to the other. You may have to provide a temporary changing room.

Define the acting area with some device such as a carpet shape, hay bales or a row of plants. Be inventive with your lighting sources, using lamps or candles as well as theatrical lighting.

It is important that you use materials and structures that will withstand wind, rain and other weather, and are tough enough to be used by the members of the audience.

At the same time you should try to use those that are appropriate to your site. Mask a garden stage with screens of potted plants or trees. Use bricks or stones to define auditorium shapes. Choose fabrics patterned in the style of the surrounding architecture. In all your design decisions try to match the character of your chosen site.

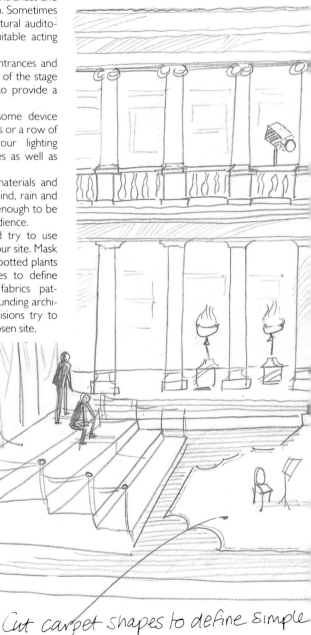

Rostra used as seating

Cut carpet shapes to define simple

Performers'
entrance

Ticket
entrance.

tage area.

27

CHAPTER 2

INTRODUCING SCENERY

THE BOX SET

A box set is a setting designed to simulate an enclosed room. It is entirely made up of one sort of scenic element – flats.

Flats – wooden frames covered in canvas cloth and painted – are the standard struc-

tures in this scenery. If they must withstand rough treatment they are covered instead with hardboard (Masonite) or thin plywood. This sort of covering is important too if the flat has a doorway in or adjacent to it. Canvas will flap unconvincingly when shaken by a closing door.

When a complicated shape like an archway

is formed by joining together several flats it is called a *French flat*. How it is constructed will be decided by your technical director or carpenter, but ask for a vertical join; it's less noticable than a horizontal one.

Flats need not be regular rectangles. An added edging shape forms a *profile flat*. If a profile flat is used to hide the bottom of a cloth or a batten of lights it is called a *groundrow*.

Flats can have a number of structural additions set into them. Note the illusion of thickness round the openings to these doors and windows; these narrow pieces are called *reveals*.

Subsidiary flats placed at right angles to the main structure are called *returns*.

Two flats hinged together form a *book flat (two-fold)*. Flats built in this way are easily stored.

SUPPORTING FLAT SCENERY

Flat scenery can be self-supporting if set at right angles and nailed together but there are other ways of holding it up.

Weights and braces
A simple telescopic brace, its length adjusted by the wing screw on its side, is hooked into a screw-eye in the back of the flat. A stage weight, shaped to fit over the foot of the brace, provides the fixture. This is a standard device for temporary support of flats.

Stage screws
The foot of the brace has a hole in it. A large screw like this can be put through it, replacing the cumbersome stage weight, if the stage floor will allow it.

French braces
Sometimes it is useful to have a wooden brace fixed permanently to the back of the scenic piece. This, called a French brace, has stage weights placed across its foot for support. French braces are useful in scene

changes and when added to flown scenery. They are hinged, and can be folded back for easy storage.

Cleat lines
A rope attached to the back of the scenery is flicked over a cleat hook on an adjacent piece, pulled tight and wound back round a similar hook in the first flat. This simple method in the hands of experts allows quick assembly and dismantling of complicated arrangements of tall flats.

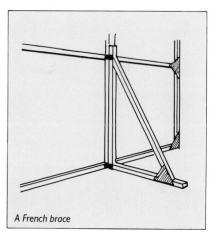

A French brace

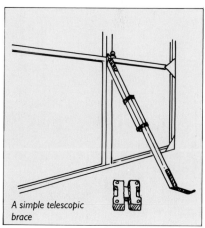

A simple telescopic brace

A ROSTRUM (PARALLEL) SETTING

Many settings need not be surrounded with walls; they can be completely made up of rostra (parallels), which produce a very dramatic acting area and emphasize the performers' use of space. Their sculptural quality can be dramatized and coloured through lighting, and they offer a very flexible way of providing multiple scenes.

This rostrum setting is made up of a small number of different three-dimensional scenic elements.

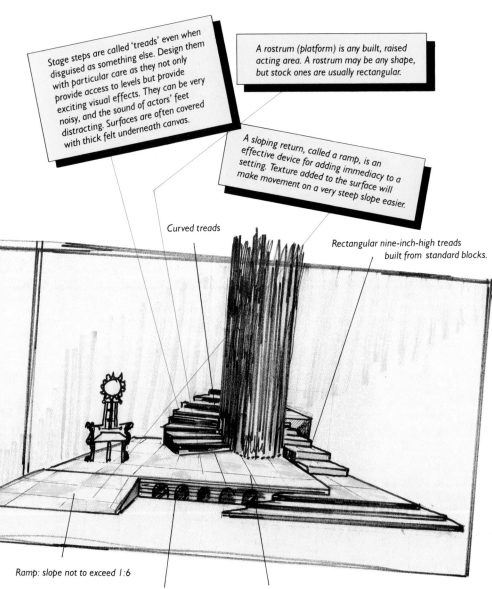

Stage steps are called 'treads' even when disguised as something else. Design them with particular care as they not only provide access to levels but provide exciting visual effects. They can be very noisy, and the sound of actors' feet distracting. Surfaces are often covered with thick felt underneath canvas.

A rostrum (platform) is any built, raised acting area. A rostrum may be any shape, but stock ones are usually rectangular.

A sloping return, called a ramp, is an effective device for adding immediacy to a setting. Texture added to the surface will make movement on a very steep slope easier.

Curved treads

Rectangular nine-inch-high treads built from standard blocks.

Ramp: slope not to exceed 1:6

Painted facing

Rostrum level: can be made up of more than one rostrum.

SOFT SCENERY

In many shows the setting is made up solely of cloth scenery. Backcloths, wings and borders, when skilfully painted, will create a total illusion and describe a location perfectly. The extra space created by this form makes it particularly suitable for ballet and musical shows. A flown cloth set is ideal in a production with many scene changes.

Back cloth

Cut cloth

Soft profile legs

Cut cloth

Profile legs

Borders placed at an appropriate height hide what is stored in the area above the stage.

Variety can be added to a setting by cutting shapes and holes in cloths and giving more depth to a scene by disclosing further distant views.

Magical and useful effects can be created with special open-weave theatrical fabrics called gauzes (scrims).

Legs are narrow, vertical pieces of soft scenery that hide people in the wings.

The backcloth is a cloth hung behind a built setting. Using a single colour or a pattern can be as effective as a complicated view by a scene painter.

CLOTHS AND GAUZES (SCRIMS)

■ The traditional scenic backcloth is a very useful device. It can provide a setting by itself or can add a vista behind an architectural scene. Cloths are of many different materials and are fireproofed. Their fibres and weaves vary according to the effects desired and how the cloth is to be stored, on stage and on tour.

A company supplying material for a backcloth will also sew it to size, adding ties at the top and a pocket with a chain for weighting at the bottom. It is possible to imitate their skill and sew your own soft scenery but the scale of the job is daunting.

A backcloth is normally lit from the front, but you can put the light source behind it and, if it is of a lightweight material, give your scene a very magical, luminous quality. A cloth lit in this way is usually painted with aniline dye. Mix front lighting on the backcloth with a moon-box illuminated at the rear to get another special illusion.

You should decide what your backcloth needs to be made of from the various types shown here. Any supplier will give you a sample catalogue of fabrics.

TYPES OF CLOTH FOR PAINTED BACKCLOTHS

GAUZES

Gauzes (scrims) have two purposes – to soften a visual effect or to make something appear and disappear magically.

A little light on a gauze hung in front of a brightly lit cyclorama or cloth will cast a misty effect over it. This makes the painted scene appear more distant. Coloured light and cloud shapes projected on the gauze can produce great varieties of atmosphere.

Moving the light source from the front of a gauze to the rear makes actors or scenery behind it appear as if by magic. The effect works best with a thicker gauze (see the types illustrated below) when it has been painted.

How a vision gauze works.

When light is projected on to the face of the gauze (scrim) the unlit actor behind it will be invisible until the illumination is taken from the front and put on the actor. The picture on the gauze disappears with no light on it.

If a grey or white fabric is used the light bouncing on to the back of it can cast a milky sheen over the illusion. You can eliminate this by carefully painting the back of the gauze with a thin black paint. You should also keep the surfaces behind it as dark as possible.

How a Gauze works:

Lit from here it seems opaque.

Lit from here, and now transparent, it reveals the actor.

Vision gauze is lighter and used mainly for misty effects and supporting cut cloths.

Sharkstooth gauze is the most opaque and will make for complete disappearing effects.

Square mesh gauze is good for transformation effects.

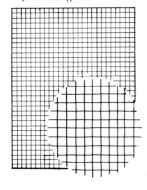

FLYING SYSTEMS AND TECHNIQUES

HEMP SETS

The simplest type of flying system is manually operated and is called a *hemp set*, as it consists of thick ropes threaded through pulleys in the theatre grid. The ropes are guided to the flying gallery in the wings and tied to a large cleat hook. When operated they are untied and lowered together, which often calls for considerable strength, skill and the services of more than one flyman.

Hemp sets have the advantage of being separate lines that can be used individually or in groups of two or three. You can tie them directly to your scenic element or fix them to a wooden batten and hang your cloth or flat from that.

'Giving a dead'.

The hemp ropes or *lines* are named by their positions away from the fly gallery. The farthest is called the *long*, next comes the *centre* and finally the *short line*. The terms are used when instructing the flyman on altering the level of a backcloth. You will be clearly understood if you ask for an adjustment 'up on the long' or 'down on the short'. This is the universal language for 'giving a dead', as fixing a scenic position is called.

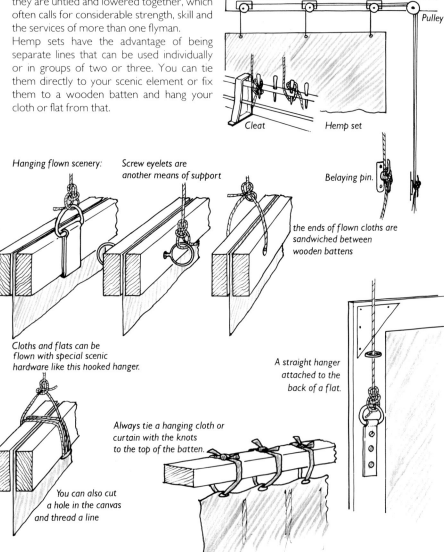

Pulley

Cleat

Hemp set

Belaying pin.

Hanging flown scenery:

Screw eyelets are another means of support

the ends of flown cloths are sandwiched between wooden battens

Cloths and flats can be flown with special scenic hardware like this hooked hanger.

A straight hanger attached to the back of a flat.

Always tie a hanging cloth or curtain with the knots to the top of the batten.

You can also cut a hole in the canvas and thread a line

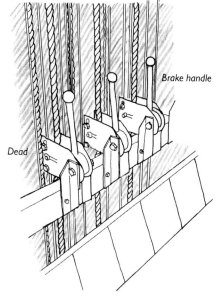

Brake handle

Dead

COUNTERWEIGHT SYSTEMS

A counterweight flying system is more complex and allows heavier scenery to be hung. Not ropes but steel wires pass through the pulleys and are permanently attached to metal pipes running the width of the stage.

The wires run from the grid to cradles in metal frames fixed to the wall. Special weights are loaded into these to counterbalance the scenery attached on stage, so that it can be hauled out easily by one flyman, who applies a brake from the fly gallery to hold the scenery in position.

Backcloths or flats are attached to the permanent metal bars by *drift lines*, which can be ropes or wires, depending on the weight to be hung.

Full flying height

So that the very tallest scenery will disappear when flown out, the fly tower above the stage must be more than twice the height of the proscenium arch. Where a complete disappearance of the backcloths is possible a stage is said to have *full flying height*.

HANGING FLOWN SCENERY

Flying wire of heavy-gauge steel is for the safe hanging of scenery. It must be attached as shown here with clips and a special fixing spanner.

The *flying irons* in this drawing are screwed to the back of built scenery to allow invisible attachment of flying wire.

Sandbags like these are tied to unused hemp lines to prevent the lines slipping through the pulleys.

These *flying weights* are shaped to fit their cradle and differ greatly from stage weights.

Counterweight set

Wire

Wire

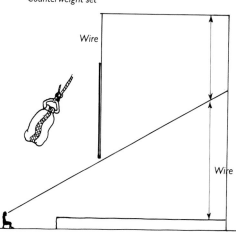

Full flying height is when you fly the tallest pieces of scenery out of view of the audience without having to fold or 'trip' them.

CHAPTER 3

DESIGNING A SET

Designing a set is rather more than putting a pretty picture on stage. It is essentially problem-solving aimed at helping the drama to unfold. If a set design also adds mood, atmosphere, character and visual spectacle it is a good one. Problems to be solved fall into three groups:

■ making the play happen
■ mechanics of the design
■ enhancing the action.

MAKING THE PLAY HAPPEN

The designer's prime purpose is to ensure that the dramatic action will be to greatest effect, so you must decide what the actors need and provide it as conveniently as you can. Listing requirements such as doors, chairs, windows and so on, with indications of how they must be used, needs great care and some dramatic insight, and placing them to best advantage on stage is is a skilful business:

■ an ill-placed door can ruin an important entrance
■ a chair placed inconveniently can inhibit an acted conversation
■ a window wrongly placed can lose conviction that it is in, say, an upstairs room.

MECHANICS OF THE DESIGN

There are many practical constraints on the

designer that lie outside the script but must be borne in mind:

■ what are the limitations of the stage to be used?
■ what will the budget permit?
■ what are the resources of the workshops?
■ how many stage staff will be available?

There is a lot to think about. It is looked at in greater detail elsewhere in this book.

ENHANCING THE ACTION

As a designer you will want to embody some dramatic interpretation in what you create, and in fact it is this aspect that makes a setting become a design. There are several ways for the designer to enhance the play:

■ accurate historical detail tells an audience exactly where and when the action is taking place
■ carefully chosen colours, forms and textures will infuse mood into a location and 'personality' into scenic elements
■ visual devices like false perspective or exaggerated light and shade can make things seem deeper, taller, farther off or more massive than the stage would allow in reality.

Without such imaginative techniques a design is dull and unexciting, but they must be married to what the actors need and the workshop can provide.

All stage design problems are interdependent. Any solution in one area must take account of the other two. That is why there is no standard way to design a play. You will learn to juggle design elements so that they project your imaginative concepts while solving the problems.

HOW TO BEGIN: DECIDING WHAT HAPPENS

Before you can start you must have a clear idea of what is actually going to happen in the play. Only when you are certain that you know how the action proceeds can you make the right visual choices. Make sure that you are entirely familiar with the text, so that you can make decisions about what you should provide, and how your design ideas will enhance the action.

THE SCRIPT

The primary source for all decisions about what is to happen in the production is, of course, the script. Careful reading will show most of what you need to know. The script should become a constant reference point to which you will return time and again. When a solution seems totally impossible, the important rule is 'return to the script.' It will be the starting point for a new train of thought, even if it does not provide an answer straight away.

Learn to visualize as you read, seeing in your mind's eye all the things that the characters refer to or use. Keep asking yourself simple questions, such as:

- where did he come from?
- where did she go to?
- how many cups are there on the table?
- what time of day is it?
- how many chairs are there?
- what number of rooms lead off this one?

The questions may seem obvious, but the answers are sometimes surprising.

Some details are hidden in the text. They may be revealed only in the dialogue, when a character refers to them. Sometimes they are there solely by inference, not actually mentioned, but nonetheless needed for the dialogue to work in action. Great care is needed to identify these items and to decide how important they are.

At the end of an initial reading you should have a list of all the items which are *essential* – that is those which are actually used or mentioned by the actors.

STAGE DIRECTIONS

An obvious place to look for information about set details is in the author's stage directions. Some writers describe what they see as the setting for the action in great detail. However, you should read them with caution. They are often used by playwrights to evoke a picture in the mind's eye during the first reading of a script. Frequently they contain descriptions of unnecessary scenic elements, and are there to evoke atmosphere and not to further the action.

Sometimes stage directions are taken from the prompt copy of the original production. This accounts for contradictory statements about actors' movements, and suggestions for superfluous furniture.

The best approach is to regard stage directions as a guide to what might be desirable, rather than an indication of what is essential. Feel completely free to discard everything you judge to be unnecessary.

INTERPRETATION

It is not only the script that determines what will happen on the stage. The action described by the author has to be interpreted by the actors, under the director's instruction. You will not be able to tackle the design without knowing what emphasis your collaborators are going to use to colour the action.

Only when discussions about this have taken place can you be said to have the whole text of the play. The script provides the basic structure, but the show is only defined in performance. The whole text is provided by the author's words, and the interpretation aimed for by the particular production. With this, the designer can start work.

INTERPRETING THE SCRIPT

A CASE STUDY

The first act of Humperdinck's opera is set in a woodcutter's cottage, where children play while their parents are out. When their mother returns she is angry that Gretel has done no work and Hansel has spilt the last of the precious milk. Furious, she sends the children out into the forest to gather berries for supper. When their father returns with food and money earned in the town he is dismayed. There is a witch in the wood, he says, known to steal children and eat them. Father and mother hurry out to search for Hansel and Gretel.

Meanwhile, in the depths of the forest, the children realize they are lost; tired and frightened, they say their prayers and fall asleep.

Next morning they are awoken by the witch, Rosina Daintymouth, who shows them her home, a gingerbread house covered with sugar and surrounded by gingerbread figures. The witch soon has Hansel in a cage to fatten him before turning him into a sweetmeat; Gretel is forced to do housework, but eventually helps her brother to escape. They push their captor into her own stove, there is an enormous explosion and all the gingerbread figures turn back into the children they once were. The opera ends with mother and father finding all the children and leading them happily home.

INTERPRETATIONS

Though the plot of this operatic folk tale is simple it could be presented in several ways: simply as a fairy tale with magic events and a happy ending; as a morality play about the corruption of innocence by evil; or as a warning against greed or neglect of duty. It could even be done as a play about children maturing by encountering a hostile outside world.

There are many different approaches for a director and his team when mounting a production, and for the designer the question of interpretation is crucial. You cannot start work until you have both the original script and an interpretative emphasis agreed with the director. How to present the opera will be decided at your preliminary meetings with the director, and all the work that follows will be based on that decision, so the first talks must be direct and specific. At the end of them you should have an outline of the implications of the chosen approach. From then on you will both seek acting, design and production methods to put across your chosen theme.

Two different approaches to the opera will show the importance of interpretation.

THE SIMPLE FAIRY TALE

A strong storyline is the main component in this tradition and the production must emphasize that, so your job is very like that of a narrator. A good storyteller provides all the necessary information economically and directly.

For the story to move briskly you must ensure that each location can be instantly recognized. The woodcutter's cottage is a scene of poverty, yet a secure and happy home. Your set details might include a large fireplace, home-made furniture, a bird cage, jars of wild flowers, sparkling pots and pans. The more simple peasant comforts you show the clearer the picture will be, drawing the audience instantly into the story.

Another reason for such detail is that the cosy scene emphasizes the children's dismay at being sent into the cold dark forest; at the end it helps the audience to share the the parents' and children's relief and joy when all return safely. Making such points clear helps to draw the emotional subtext supporting the storytelling.

Rosina's cottage should be designed as mouthwateringly as possible, a delightful confection, covered in sweet things, that will tell the audience how the witch so easily lured the sweet-toothed children inside. Your design will explain, without any long speeches, how the trap has worked on previous victims, and the reappearing children in place of gingerbread figures at the climax of the story at once become understandable. Once again the design does the narrating. It even explains what has been happening before the action starts.

In designing to this brief you must draw your

details directly from the storyline and choose them for their directness in furthering the plot. Unambiguous shapes and colours, easily recognized objects, are essential. Any distortion you use must make set details *more* recognizable so that the story unfolds clearly and simply.

THE MORALITY PLAY

Mounting the opera as a moral tale of innocence corrupted by evil means quite different design decisions. You must create images to draw the audience's attention to the moral theme behind the folk tale. You will be seeking set details whose qualities contrast good with evil, the wholesomeness of the woodcutter's cottage with the invisible evil forces of the forest.

For example the cottage might display religious objects – a bible, an ikon or a crucifix. The lighting could be by candles to suggest a church-like atmosphere. The architectural details might also suggest church arches and heavy wooden doors. Colours and textures – plain oak furniture and whitewashed walls – would hint at a plain, almost puritan lifestyle. Every detail should be associable with purity and innocence.

In the forest scene you can make good use of the visual 'personalities' of objects – tall spiky conifers with sharp needles, dead branches pointing dagger-like at the children, sinister black holes in tree trunks.

The witch's gingerbead house lets you combine connotations with personality effects. The sugary-sweet elements that entice the innocent children can also have a disturbing appearance. Spires on the roof and barley sugar window bars can be made to look sharp and dangerous, and the whole house can loom menacingly over and round the glowing oven, sweets and toffees casting menacing shadows. You might even make the gingerbread figures look stern and soldier-like. Everything can have connotations of sweetness but the personality of evil. Exaggerated candy colours could be used to good effect.

To sum up, your design details must all underline the production theme, painting a picture of God-fearing innocents confronting evil forces, falling into a corrupting trap but finally triumphing.

The Children's Home: a design stressing the play's moral overtones.

The Witch's Cottage: a fairy tale design.

39

THE DESIGNER'S GRID – A MAP OF THE PLAY

It is helpful to make notes about the text of the play as reminders of essential design points. Underlining places in your script is a useful start but making a designer's grid from this information will give you an overview of the piece and help you to see where scene changes are necessary – or difficult. With every problem put in its context the structure of the play should become clear. Having the information so concisely ensures that you do not overlook anything you will have to provide.

DESIGN CHART AND ANALYSIS FOR "TWELFTH NIGHT" by William Shakespeare

ACT	SCENE	TIME	LOCATION	CHARACTERS IN SCENE	TEXT NOTES		ANALYSIS
I	1	?	Orsino's Palace	3(+)	Music playing (musicians onstage?)	A	**A** Second major location ORSINOS PALACE Are the musicians seen, necessary or desirable?
	2	?	Sea shore?	2(+)	Characters shipwrecked	B	**B**
	3	?	Olivia's House (Illyria)	3	House of "Virtuous maid" in 12 month mourning for dead brother, has "abjured the sight & company of men" DANCING TAKES PLACE IN SCENE	C	**C**
	4	?	Orsino's Palace	3(+)		A	**C** MAJOR SCENE OLIVIAS HOUSE No reference to furniture – could be GARDEN? this would give access for officers who arrest Sebastian and clown who drifts between the houses. NB. hiding place, and drinking scene which may require furniture
	5	?	Olivia's House	5(+)	Viola – "At the gate"?	D	
II	1	?	Town Street?	2		C	
	2		Olivia's House	2			
	3	Post mid-night	Olivia's House	5	Drinking scene – "Do you make an ale house of my mistress' House?" Singing, dancing	A	
	4	Morning	Orsinos Palace	5+	Music again	C	
	5	Sunny day	Olivia's House	4	Hiding place for 3 people	C	
III	1	?	Olivia's House	6		C	
	2	?	Olivia's House	3		D	**B AND D** Third location – could be the same unspecified area
	3		Town Street?	2		C	
	4		Olivia's House	5	Hiding place for 3 people sword fight and ARREST	C	
IV	1		Olivia's House	6	Sword fight	C	
	2		Olivia's House	4	PRISON FOR MALVOLIO He can hear but not see his tormentor – in darkness	C	
	3	Sunny day	Olivia's House	3		C	
V	1		Olivia's House	8+	Full cast on stage	C	

THE MECHANICS OF A DESIGN

PREPARING A GROUND PLAN

Designing for the actor

Start your design by working out your ground plan. This is your foundation and will have a determining effect on the whole production. A ground plan is really a design for the action, and your aim here must be to help the actors in their work. Try to create a plan containing all the elements you have identified as necessary and allowing the players to move about comfortably. Also, by exploiting the theatrical effectiveness of certain stage positions, you can place actors so as to enhance their dramatic roles. Remember – a bad ground plan can destroy actors' work.

STAGE POSITIONS

To help actors you must know how they use the stage and the language they employ. When actors are near the audience they say they are 'downstage'. When they move towards the back they move 'upstage'. The terms derive from the old stages that sloped down from back to front. Remembering this will keep them clear in your mind.

The terms 'onstage', 'offstage' and 'centre-stage' are familiar and self-explanatory, but confusion arises over 'stage left' and 'stage right'. Try to remember that left and right are always *the actors'* left and right as they face the audience, the opposite of what the audience sees.

You should be able to locate DSR (downstage right) CF (centre front), UL (upstage left) and all the variations of these positions by their shorthand terms. This way of saying where things happen will be used by everyone in the production.

Other terms are used by designers to describe the positions of scenery and furniture. A piece that runs 'on and off' is placed parallel with the front of the stage. Similarly a flat placed 'up and down stage' is at a right-angle to the audience.

When scenery was transported from theatre to theatre by repertory companies its position on stage was marked on the back. The usual practice was to mark the piece nearest the prompt corner PS1, (prompt side, first piece) and so on until the centre was reached, while scenery for the other side of the stage was marked OP (opposite prompt). To avoid confusion the prompt side was always stage left, even if a particular theatre had an unusual prompt corner on stage right. The terms PS and OP are used less frequently now that touring is less popular but they do occur.

Stage Positions:

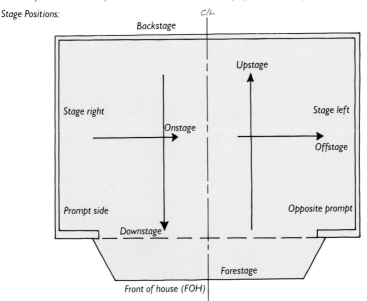

Backstage

Upstage

Stage right

Stage left

Onstage

Offstage

Prompt side

Opposite prompt

Downstage

Forestage

Front of house (FOH)

SIGHTLINES

Your first step in preparing a ground plan is to determine what part of the stage can be seen by the whole audience. Start with the printed ground plan supplied by the theatre. This shows mainly stage detail, but you will also find vital information about the auditorium. Look for points marked by crosses. They represent viewing positions of people sitting in the outermost seats.

By drawing lines from these points or continuing those already drawn you can determine exactly what lies within the sightline of every member of the audience. They must pass just inside the obstruction of the proscenium arch or anything else blocking the view. The actors can be seen in the area downstage of these lines and this acting area is where you will design your setting. You can put decorative elements outside it but only if they are not essential to the action.

Check what can be seen from the outside limits of the seating whenever you add a set element to the ground plan. Sometimes you will be ensuring that the actor can be seen; at other times you may be trying to hide the actor. A player invisible to anyone in the audience is 'masked'.

An actor only partly obscured, by a low wall for instance, will still be at a disadvantage, being unable to kneel or lie down for long and suffering the psychological effect of being half hidden. An audience feels estranged from an actor who is not fully in view.

STRONG AND WEAK POSITIONS

You will soon learn that some places on stage are more commanding than others. This is valuable, when making ground plan decisions, in ensuring that important entrances are strong.

The strongest place for a player is just where the upstage sightlines cross, which commands anyone else on stage as well as the auditorium. With hardly a turn of the head the actor can see and talk to anyone else on stage while facing the audience. The other actors have to face upstage to reply, weakening their own contact with the audience.

The strength of a player's position on stage therefore depends on two factors: being upstage of other actors and facing the audience.

Moving downstage and offstage, left or right, away from the upstage centre point, progressively weakens the actor. Even when still in a superior position at the apex of a triangle of actors but he or she will be less able to face the audience comfortably.

You will find it useful to think of all acting positions in terms of triangles. A director tries to place actors in these geometrical groups wherever they are acting on stage. Triangular formations form natural positions of strength and weakness and also help to prevent actors masking each other.

SIGHTLINES FOR UNCONVENTIONAL STAGES

Even when you design for a theatre with an unconventionally shaped stage you will be applying the same principles. An actor's strongest position on stage is at the intersection of the sightlines and when his or her view engages most of the audience.

Theatre-in-the-round

The crossing point in theatre-in-the-round is obviously at the centre of the stage, but from there an actor cannot engage *most* of the audience without turning round on the spot. However, a move towards any corner of the stage can form triangular positions with the other actors and encompass most of the audience. The people remaining behind the actor must be engaged as fellow protagonists.

This is an important principle for designing 'in the round'. The audience must feel itself psychologically in touch with the actors even from behind. Masking or half-masking pieces of set need to be very carefully considered.

Thrust stages

Here there are two focal points, one far upstage and one right downstage; both are drawn from the sightlines of a majority of the audience. The actor's place in either spot commands the rest of the playing area and also most of the auditorium. Again the actor at either point must be able to engage the viewers who are seated behind.

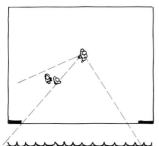

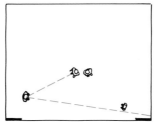

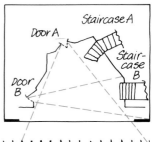

The actor is in a strong position because he can easily keep the audience and the other actors within his eyeline.

Here the actor's position is weak because he cannot keep the audience in his sight when addressing the other players.

Door A is in a strong position because an actor entering through it has the audience and everyone on stage immediately in his sightline. Door B does not allow this and so is weaker. Compare Staircase A with Staircase B similarly.

Sightlines:

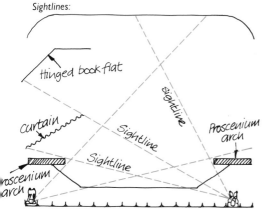

Dotted lines show sightlines from the outer extremes of the seating. Viewers can see everything between these lines. The advantage of using angled wing curtains, a curved cyclorama or a hinged book flat is clearly seen.

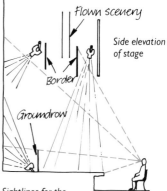

Sightlines for the front-row audience. In limiting the sightline the groundrow and border hide the lamps lighting the scenery, and actors and the stored scenery in the flies.

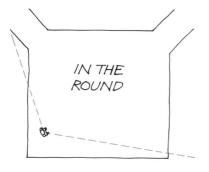

Theatre in the round: a strong position can never encompass all the audience. The actor must use other techniques.

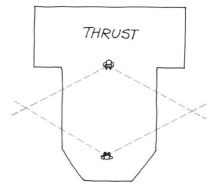

Two strong positions of the thrust stage.

FURNITURE IN A SETTING

Your script will give you ideas about placing your furniture but remember that you are trying to do two things:

■ put the actors in their most effective stage positions and
■ help them move about the stage.

So it is important that you find out what the action requires in terms of both furniture and empty spaces. Start by making a rough sketch of what you think would be the best arrangement, then ask yourself some questions:

■ what is the balance between furniture and open space?

Arrange your furniture in groups and balance them with open spaces, taking care not to make either too large. A too-big open space can look artificial and lead to too much striding about. Tables and chairs are usually grouped for a specific function – eating, writing or conversation. By defining the role for each furniture group you will arrive at its natural shape and size.

■ are the entrances clear?

Actors do not want to walk round chairs to enter. They need to get directly into the main acting area.

Furniture in a setting:
The placing of furniture stresses the relationships in the scene. Here each grouping of a table and two chairs suggests a dramatic situation.

■ are there good movement diagonals?

Check that an actor can move about without having to go round a piece of furniture. You should be able to draw quite long lines from area to area or chair to chair, routes that – especially when they help diagonal moves across the stage – are very strong and useful to the director. For that reason avoid placing furniture in a straight line across the stage. It blocks the diagonal paths and makes for very dull action.

■ what are the sightlines like?

Place the furniture so that no one will be masked by any of it or by another actor.

■ will the actor be able to 'include' the audience easily?

Remember the players' need to command a view of the audience and so include them in the dramatic action. An actor seated in a chair that makes him face upstage loses this vital contact. Aim to provide positions from

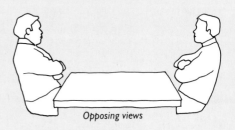

Opposing views

A friendly discussion

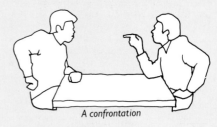

A confrontation

Boss and worker

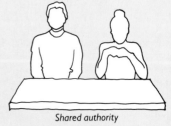

Shared authority

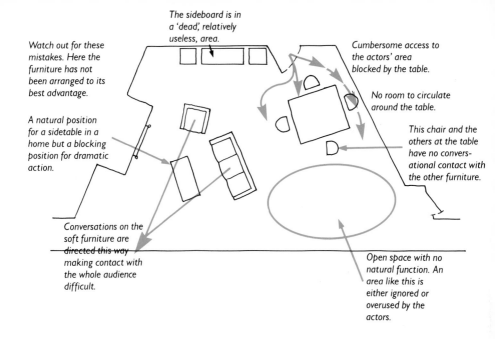

The sideboard is in a 'dead', relatively useless, area.

Watch out for these mistakes. Here the furniture has not been arranged to its best advantage.

Cumbersome access to the actors' area blocked by the table.

No room to circulate around the table.

A natural position for a sidetable in a home but a blocking position for dramatic action.

This chair and the others at the table have no conversational contact with the other furniture.

Conversations on the soft furniture are ~~directed this way~~ making contact with the whole audience difficult.

Open space with no natural function. An area like this is either ignored or overused by the actors.

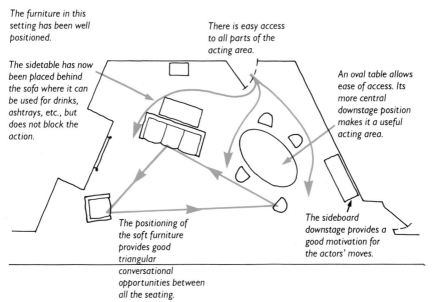

The furniture in this setting has been well positioned.

There is easy access to all parts of the acting area.

The sidetable has now been placed behind the sofa where it can be used for drinks, ashtrays, etc., but does not block the action.

An oval table allows ease of access. Its more central downstage position makes it a useful acting area.

The positioning of the soft furniture provides good triangular conversational opportunities between all the seating.

The sideboard downstage provides a good motivation for the actors' moves.

which actors can comfortably engage the attention of both the audience and each other.

You may accidentally produce an area in which actors will feel uneasy while playing. This can happen if furniture cuts a space off, making it hard to use without a long or indirect route. Large tables, badly placed, are the usual cause; once in behind one an actor can find it hard to get back in the action. A shift in the angle of the offending piece, allowing a more direct route out, may be the answer.

■ how natural does it look?

ENTRANCES AND EXITS

Good entrances are very important to actors, and where you place the doors in your set will strongly affect the impression they make as they appear on stage.

As designer you have to judge exactly what impact should be made.

Remember too that a character's exit is sometimes the climax of his or her action on stage. Do not ruin it by providing an awkward or clumsy way out.

Read your script carefully once again and ask:

■ how many entrances do I need?

List all the entrances and exits used or referred to and decide which are necessary. Be economical. It may be hard to find suitable positions for too many. Even a domestic setting may not need a door for every room indicated. One can lead to a corridor with several rooms off it, or an open arch can give access to more than one room.

■ where should the entrances be placed?

Treat them like actors. For strong effects place them upstage centre. The more off-centre and the farther downstage an entrance the less dominant, and more 'vulnerable' it is. Like actors, entrances gain dramatic force when in 'full-face' control over the acting and auditorium areas. They become passive when focused away from either.

If you are designing for a play that requires several settings, try to plan some variety in entrances so that actors are not forced into repetitious movements.

With this in mind, together with your ideas about the shape of the action, you will be able to place effective entrances. But you must remember the architectural reality of the notional building round your setting. Ask yourself where an architect would put the rooms. Draw a sketch plan of the whole imaginary building. It will reveal errors and suggest new layouts.

Even outdoor scenes need this kind of thinking. It should be quite clear to the audience what the topography of the surrounding (notional) landscape is. Use a sketch map to decide what entrance positions suggest it best.

■ which way does the door open?

In the theatre a door is described by the way it opens. If a door is hinged on its upstage edge and swings offstage it opens 'upstage and off', and one opposite in both respects is said to open 'downstage and on'. Combinations of these terms are used by everyone to indicate briefly how to build or use a door.

The sizes and shapes of your doors will depend on the dramatic or social milieu of the play, but how a door opens can determine how an entrance is made. Consider these examples:

This door opens upstage and off, revealing the actor immediately. But the actor has to take a step back to draw it towards him so his entrance is delayed by a beat. An *exit* through this door would be quick and forceful.

Opening upstage and on, this door allows for a sudden and immediate entrance on stage. Notice the masking problems upstage of the door.

A door opening downstage and on gives an actor a great opportunity for a furtive, 'Peeping-Tom' entrance but exit will be slow because the door is pulled on stage.

Here the actor is revealed suddenly in the doorway and an exit will be very speedy, but the backing needs special attention.

You may want to use the 'bursting' effect of double doors like these, opening on stage, but remember that an exit through them is necessarily slow even with a self-closing mechanism.

Double doors opening off stage make for a very grand appearance, but stepping back to draw the doors towards you means an entrance more stately than sudden.

■ can I have steps up to a door?

You will sometimes want to reinforce the effect of a door by placing it at the top of some stairs. If you do this remember to provide a landing on either side. Otherwise it is almost impossible for actors not to stumble on the stairs as they draw the door towards themselves or push it open.

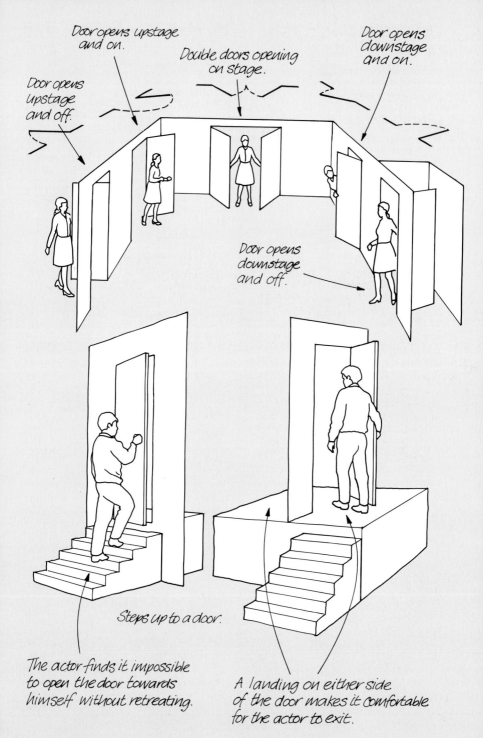

Door opens upstage and on.

Door opens upstage and off.

Double doors opening on stage.

Door opens downstage and on.

Door opens downstage and off.

Steps up to a door.

The actor finds it impossible to open the door towards himself without retreating.

A landing on either side of the door makes it comfortable for the actor to exit.

THE IMPORTANCE OF LEVELS

There are many advantages in varying the heights of the different acting areas on your ground plan. Differing levels can:

■ define and separate acting areas
■ give characters positions of hierarchy and dominance
■ enable actors to be grouped effectively so that they can all be seen, none masking any other
■ give the chorus members in musical theatre a clear view of the conductor.

If you decide to use levels on your ground plan bear in mind that:

■ you will have to design not only the levels but also access to them from stage level, using stairs and ramps
■ you must provide areas and access stairs large enough for the actors to feel safe and comfortable while using them
■ you need a good balance between acting and access areas so that, say, no actor has to play on a flight of steps with one foot higher than the other
■ an upper level with only one access prevents characters leaving unobtrusively without re-entering the main acting area and a director will usually ask for another means of escape, so always provide two routes up to a level.

DESIGNING ACCESS STEPS

When you draw up a ground plan with levels remember that steps take up a lot of space. Each tread (the surface you step on) should be at least a foot wide. The riser (the height of the step) should be from six to nine inches high for comfortable use – certainly no higher than a foot. For safety the steps should be about as wide as a door.

Thus to provide steps to a height of six feet you need an area measuring about two foot-six inches by five feet. Calculate carefully. You may have to use ingenious bends and turns to get your access into the available space.

HOW HIGH CAN LEVELS BE?

An actor can seem quite high up without actually being far above stage level. Height is relative on stage, being largely defined by the eye contact of the players. An actor standing two feet higher than another will dominate, looking down yet still engaging the eye. On a four-foot-high rostrum that actor will almost lose the contact unless he or she bends or leans forward, and the other actor must stand some distance away, making conversation remote. Above this height natural eye contact is lost and they can appear quite separated.

There are, of course, many theatrical ways of manipulating this phenomenon but the important point is that you can give an impression of great height without tall structures that put actors' heads up in the borders.

DEFINING AREAS WITH LEVELS

You can use levels to define and separate areas on stage, doing away with walls or other divisions. Even a four-inch change of level can indicate a different room, so you can make multiple divisions with quite low ones.

Of course, director and actors must follow your convention and not step off the level delineating a particular space. To avoid this calculate carefully the spaces required and their arrangement. Discuss and agree your ideas in detail with your director at the planning stage.

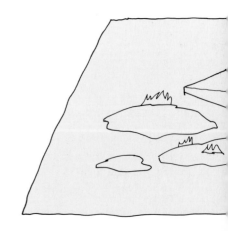

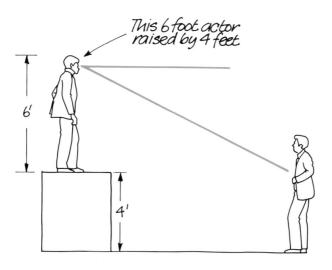

This 6 foot actor
raised by 4 feet

6'

4'

Standing at a height of 4 feet, a 6 foot tall actor is
in a very dominant position on stage. He appears
remote too because to make eye contact with him
an equally tall actor must stand a long way off.

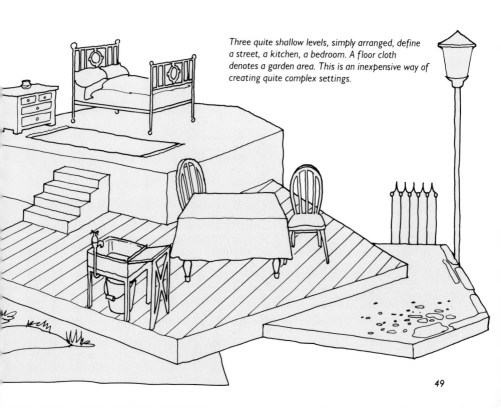

Three quite shallow levels, simply arranged, define
a street, a kitchen, a bedroom. A floor cloth
denotes a garden area. This is an inexpensive way of
creating quite complex settings.

BEYOND THE SETTING

Design carefully what you should provide *beyond* your setting. In particular plan all routes off the stage. As well as being entrances and exits, they may have to accommodate complicated scene changes so be sure that they are both convenient and safe. Some exits and scene changes will be done in darkness, and even a simple effect like having an actor disappear between black wing curtains must be worked out and drawn on your ground plan. Work from your production analysis, deciding how many people will need to use each entrance at once and ensuring them enough space to do it in comfort and safety.

BACKINGS

These practical arrangements can be made visually effective with scenic elements placed beyond the set and glimpsed through entrance doors and windows. These 'backings' let you enlarge your design and describe more of the notional environment beyond that seen on stage. With invention and imagination you can convince the audience that though characters leave the set they remain in the same dramatic world.

Some simple but effective ideas for imaginative backings.

Decide how far your backings need to extend by drawing a line from the outermost viewing point past the downstage edge of each entrance or window. This shows you how far the audience can see, its sightline. Though a simple book flat (two-fold) hinged at an angle will hide what you do not wish to be seen in the wing, you should try to do something different or more complex.

■ on backing flats use details like wallpaper, dados, picture rails to give more information
■ an architectural feature like a window, a pillar or the bottom of a flight of stairs seen through an entrance will add reality
■ a piece of furniture, a sculpture or a vase of flowers, cleverly lit against an anonymous background, can suggest the character of a space without the use of flats
■ a silhouette groundrow before a brightly lit cyclorama will make a window view more convincing
■ a gobo or other projected lighting effect on a plain backing creates an illusion of great space.

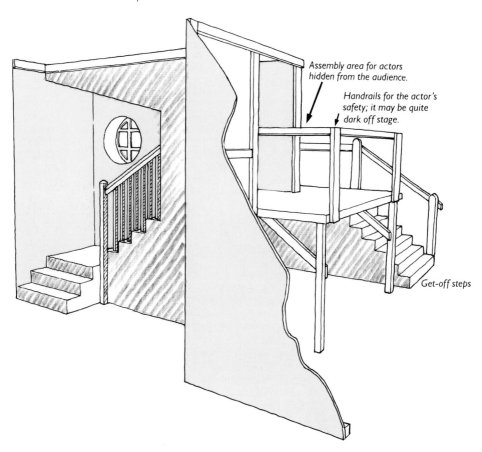

Designing Access Steps: Notice how much space may be needed for access steps.

Assembly area for actors hidden from the audience.

Handrails for the actor's safety; it may be quite dark off stage.

Get-off steps

GET-OFFS

If you design an exit at the top of a flight of stairs remember to provide a way back to stage level behind the set.

This 'get-off' must be comfortable, safe and as wide as the steps onstage, though you may be able to design it for a smaller area by using clever twists and turns. **As the light offstage is restricted a handrail is essential for safety,** and you should include an assembly area for players to prepare in before entering.

You will see that a get-off needs ample space, so allow for it on your ground plan from the outset.

ISLAND SETTINGS

A set surrounded by an open stage and apparently unconnected to the wing masking is called an 'island setting'. With this design you would probably want to contrive exits and get-offs allowing actors to leave the stage yet be concealed from view. Otherwise they must cross an expanse of open stage to exit. You must be certain that your director is happy with this arrangement. Check through the script together to be sure that he fully understands the implications of such a decision. A last-minute re-arrangement of masking could be costly and will certainly compromise your design.

CHAPTER 4

SCENE CHANGES

Scene changes in a script offer a great challenge, but before accepting one decide exactly what sort of changeable setting is wanted. There are three possibilities.

COMPLETE SET CHANGES

If you decide to have completely different sets for each location make sure that you have the means to mount them. Considerable time is needed to change a complex full setting but the audience must not be left to get bored. If the director plans long and convenient intervals you can rearrange completely what you have on stage. Otherwise you will need sophisticated equipment such as a large revolving stage, a good flying system or hydraulic lifts – and an adequate stage crew.

Plan the off-stage storage of your sets from the outset. You may need more space than you had thought! If storage space is tight you will have to use shared elements such as permanent backcloths, reversible flats, or rostra (parallels), clever use of which can save space and cut scene-changing time.

MULTIPLE SETTINGS

A multiple setting has several permanent locations on stage together. The light levels on them are raised and lowered to focus the audience's attention on any one of them. Your task is to arrange the acting spaces appropriately on stage and design each one to be recognizably distinctive.

It is important to know how often each location will be used in the play. Place the several areas very carefully on your ground plan, keeping the best acting spot, downstage centre, for the most important ones – but not putting actors into areas where audience contact is difficult, even for short scenes.

You can define the different areas in many ways – with walls, floor textures or simple furniture arrangements.

Keep your design simple. Try to decide what single colour, texture, detail or furniture characterizes each area best. Resist overdesigning; it can make a multiple setting fussy and confusing.

You may have to overlap some areas, and this will call for some ingenious design details that work for both locations.

INTEGRAL CHANGES

In this kind of setting a space is designed as atmospheric but neutral. Changes are suggested by adding elements to it. Make the permanent surround very characterful – e.g. a highly polished wooden floor, a decorative false proscenium, the theatre's bare backstage walls. You can effect many scene changes by simply bringing on different props – bushes, furniture, military equipment and so on.

More complex architectural elements – windows, doors, pillars – can be added or they can be a permanent part of the surrounding set, moved cleverly into place when required. They may revolve or slide on, or you might fly or truck them.

Whatever your basic set it must be a strong but flexible idea, perfectly evoking the atmosphere of the play. You will have to devote much preliminary thought to relevant colours, textures, materials and images, which must fit in with the different locations that your additional scenery is designed to create.

WAYS TO CHANGE A SETTING

You may become very skilful at inventing ways to change scenes, but knowing and adapting traditional devices can help you to solve many problems. Here they are just outlined; the technical details can be found elsewhere in the book.

Flying

Soft scenery such as backcloths and gauzes (scrims) can be flown out for an almost instantaneous scene change. Other scenery – doors, walls, chandeliers and so on – can be stored in the flies and added to your setting.

You can even join flown pieces to three-dimensional elements on stage – the flat, painted branches of a tree over a built trunk, for example.

Flat scenery is the easiest to fly but the available flying system will limit how much you can do.

These two photos show the same setting and the different effects that can be achieved with flown scenery.

MORE WAYS TO CHANGE A SETTING

Double-sided flats are a simple means of changing the setting.

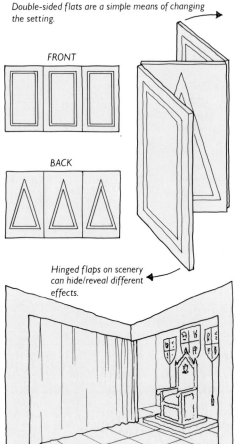

FRONT

BACK

Flats

These can be painted canvas on both sides and reversible for a quick change. They can be flipped open like a book or hinged in numerous other ways. Try sliding them out from behind each other or regrouping them to form simple combinations.

A circular curtain permits a quick change of backcloth. Here curtains are used to hide/reveal different parts of the setting.

Hinged flaps on scenery can hide/reveal different effects.

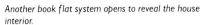

Fabric effects

Curtains can, of course, be used to hide parts of a setting, then drawn to reveal them as necessary. But they can themselves describe a location by the way they are clustered or draped, imitating tree trunks for instance.

Double-sided curtains, run on a circular track, can change a backcloth quickly. Camouflage nets or other leafy fabrics can be draped over permanent elements to disguise them as vegetation.

A translucent cloth may be stuck on the back of an opaque fabric cut to a shape. Switching the light source from front to back will produce a dramatic silhouette.

Another book flat system opens to reveal the house interior.

Trucks and wagons

Large scenic elements can be moved easily when mounted on wheels. The 'trucks' or 'wagons' have special strong casters about three inches in diameter. Remember that the wheels will raise your scenery about five inches above stage level.

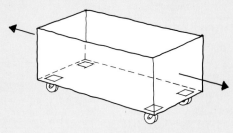

The casters may be made of plastic or rubber, plastic being cheaper but far noisier. They should not be used in view of the audience as the noise can be very distracting. The wheels are of two kinds:

Fixed wheels

These do not swivel and so are useful for moving trucks in a predetermined straight line. As the wagons are hard to move off their fixed paths you need no guide rails to ensure correct positioning. But remember this inflexibility of movement when you plan storage of this scenery offstage.

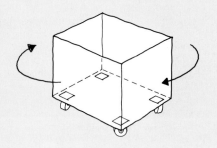

Fixed wheels are used also in constructing a revolving truck. They are placed in concentric circles round a pivot point so that their fixed direction ensures smooth rotation.

The pivot point need not be at the centre of the truck. You can use semi-circular or quarter-circle shapes with eccentric pivot points to swing scenery on stage.

Swivel wheels

These swivel independently, allowing the wagon to be freely manoeuvred on stage along a flexible path. If you want it to move along a pre-determined route you will need a shallow wooden guide rail fixed to the floor for it to run against.

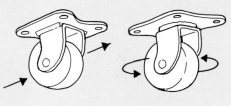

Revolving stages

Some theatres have turntables set into the stage which can be rotated mechanically to show various pre-erected scenes. They allow very quick changes and are most useful. They are sometimes to be had on hire.

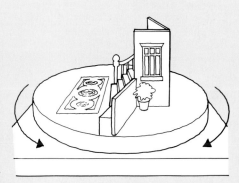

It is possible – but expensive – to build a temporary 'revolve'. If you plan to use one remember that it will be five inches off the stage floor and you may have to build up round it.

You would need to justify the expense of building a temporary revolve by using it again in subsequent plays.

PROJECTED SCENERY

Choosing projected scenery

Projection is a complex technical effect requiring much planning and preparatory work and the right equipment. But it is a useful theatrical device and, confronted with a lot of scene changes, you may be tempted to use projected scenery. You can also add projected images from relevant photographs or paintings as comments on a play's action.

But unless you consider some basic problems and follow some fundamental rules you will be disappointed with the results.

Is projection really the answer?

Any projections you plan must really help the play, particularly the actors. A projected image can be so mesmeric that it attracts disproportionate attention. Think how a TV screen in a bar or pub naturally draws the eye. Is this the effect you want?

In the illustration opposite the projected caricatures are far stronger than anything the actor below could physically present. The performances are overwhelmed by the technical effect.

In the other example the image is graphically specific but has been fragmented so that the photograph is transformed into a scenic background.

Using projections will restrict your design. You will need to make sure that the screen is big enough for impact when it is used but anonymous when it is not. You will have to accept certain colour limitations and special scenic/lighting devices to ensure a dark enough stage. Acting areas will have to be away from the screen in order not to interfere with the projections.

As you can see, a decision to use projected scenery needs to be taken with great care.

Do I have the technical resources?

To get a reasonable effect you need the right power sources, projectors, stage space and slide-making facilities. Some of these you may have already, but almost certainly you will need the money to hire equipment or buy expensive technical services.

What kind of projector should I use?

If you want a bright picture more than ten feet square you need the 5K projection lantern (lamp). It provides a very strong light source but must be fitted with a special projection lens and a slide carrier for three-inch or four-inch glass slides. Like the alternative but less powerful 2K lantern it is a standard theatrical instrument. Both need their own tripod stands and you should plan space and masking for these. They have no automatic slide-changing facility and so need an operator.

For remotely controlled slide changing you can use the standard Kodak Karousell projector. It must be fitted with an appropriate lens and an extra bright tungsten-halogen bulb. You will also need a special modification to allow fading of the light on this instrument while maintaining power for the automatic changing of the slides. Images from these projectors are smaller and less bright than those from the larger lanterns. (See lighting in this series)

Where do I project from?

You can project from in front of the screen (front-projection) or from behind it (back-projection). The farther away the lantern is the bigger the image will be, but it will also be less bright because light is lost travelling from source to screen.

Place your projector so as to avoid shadows from the actors, high enough to angle the beam over their heads. Back-projection obviates that problem, but even then you must make sure that the audience is not staring directly at your projector through the screen. The light-source will be diffused but the ugly 'hot spot' will not be eliminated.

If you project at an angle on to the screen your art work must be photographed to compensate for the effects of distortion (see LIGHTING in this series).

What kind of screen can I use?

You can project on to any surface but you will get a brighter picture if it is white or pale, if it is reflective like a special screen and if — for back-projection — it is not too opaque.

How bright will the picture be?
This depends on the power of your light source, the screen's reflectivity and what light is lost over the distance from projector to screen.

How big a picture can I get?
This is affected by the size of your lens and its distance from the screen. Here is a formula to help you calculate the screen size.

Most technical details, including decisions on preparing slides, will probably be worked out by your technical director, but he will need your ground plan to show him the size of the screen, the positions of projectors and the masking for projectors and lamps.

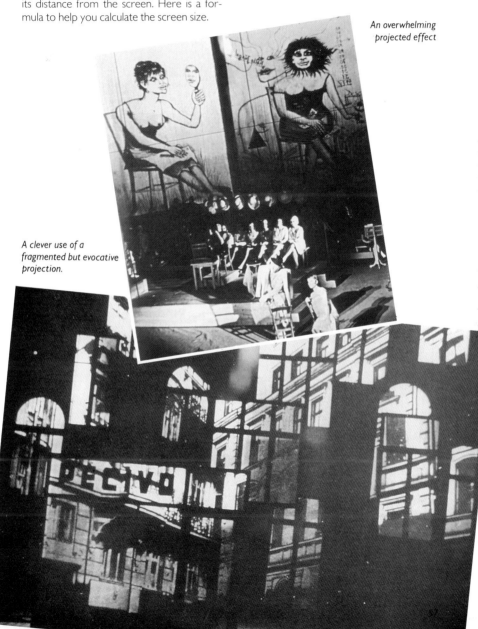

An overwhelming projected effect

A clever use of a fragmented but evocative projection.

59

Tips for a clearer image

You can ensure a bright clear picture by good designing. If extra light – perhaps originally meant to illuminate the actors – bounces on to the screen from reflective stage surfaces it will weaken the image.

Work out design features to exclude this unwanted light:

■ use dark colours in your setting
■ keep reflective surfaces, especially on the floor, to a minimum
■ baffle reflected light from the stage with a black gauze in front of the screen. This is especially useful in back-projection
■ try to include a groundrow to collect as much light from the stage as possible before it can reach the screen
■ light the actors from the side when possible, reducing damaging front light
■ give the screen a black border to sharpen the projected image by contrast.

LEGAL RESTRICTIONS

Even imagination cannot get round certain things – e.g. local bye-laws on safety and fire precautions. They vary from place to place

but you must observe the legal requirements on gangway widths, fire-proofing, aisle lighting, exits and entrances. Find out about these matters *early on*!

TOURING SHOWS

Planning round the limiting factors is important in every production, but touring shows especially need such detailed attention.

If your show is to play in more than one theatre you should try to see the ground plans of each one and work to the lowest common factors. Every theatre has its quirks, so watch out for them.

Check particularly:

■ the sizes and positions of get-in (load-in) doors
■ different sized proscenium arches, apron stages, wing spaces, etc.
■ the position of safety curtains on each stage
■ the possibility of varying the fire and safety regulations
■ unusual or inconvenient flying systems.

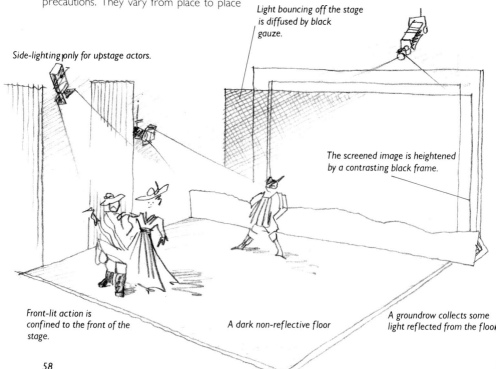

Light bouncing off the stage is diffused by black gauze.

Side-lighting only for upstage actors.

The screened image is heightened by a contrasting black frame.

Front-lit action is confined to the front of the stage.

A dark non-reflective floor

A groundrow collects some light reflected from the floor

DESIGN LIMITATIONS

In deciding what scenic devices will make the play work your imaginative response to the script is constantly checked and modified by practical considerations. So far most have been prompted by the actors' and director's needs, but several other factors impose limits. By looking at these now you can prevent your ground plan becoming a beautiful – but unrealizable – ideal.

STAGE LIMITATIONS

You have tackled some stage limitations already, sightlines and storage space for instance. Now you must get information on all the facilities available, for they will affect your design in many ways. Visit the theatre or, if that is not possible, scrutinize the stage and auditorium plans with great care. You will need the answers to a number of questions:

■ does the seating slope steeply, letting the whole audience see the stage floor?
■ is the auditorium flat, making levels on stage essential?
■ is the stage raked? If so, how steeply does it slope up towards the back?
■ is the proscenium arch very elaborate, enhancing or distracting from your intended design?
■ how high are this theatre's borders usually kept?
■ can the actors get from one side of the stage to the other quickly and easily?
■ is there a way to get from backstage to front-of-house?
■ are there any unusual physical obstructions on stage or in the wings – such as pillars, or immovable walls?

FINANCIAL LIMITATIONS

Be careful not to propose a setting which is too expensive. Study your budget, make sure that it is adequate and aim to spend just that amount.
But what is an 'adequate' budget? It is impossible to say. Broadway producers spend thousands of dollars paying union-stipulated fees and overtime rates. London theatre managements must pay for outworkers who charge a lot for their props

and painting. These conditions may or may not apply to your show.
Remember a basic rule: *Time = Money*. The more time spent on planning, preparing and making, the less things cost. Planning early means time in hand for seeking inexpensive means and materials. Money is usually overspent on solving last-minute problems that could have been avoided by thinking in advance. Do that as you prepare your ground plan.
You may have to think of low-cost solutions from the start. Do not grumble at this. The need for economies can make you synthesize your ideas. A really economical solution can be stronger and more vivid than a hundred decorative features.
For example, you may have to use cheap materials that are to hand rather than expensive traditional ones. Imaginative use of what is available can be very evocative. A heap of old tyres may conjure up a whole garage. The ribs of a ship's hold can be created with a stack of wooden pallets. Hemp flying lines lowered into view could suggest forest lianas. Clothes on a washing line will perhaps evoke an Italian village. With old doors and window frames from a demolition site you could create a town – or a palace!

WORKSHOP LIMITATIONS

remember your workshop staff. Do not ask them to build, paint, or produce too much. Even if they manage the quantity the quality will probably suffer. Ask these questions;

■ how many people are there to build the set?
■ what equipment do they have?
■ in what space is the construction and painting being done?
■ what storage space will there be for work completed or in progress?
■ what are the paintshop facilities? How much space, manpower, etc.?
■ what drying time will the proposed process need?
■ how easily does scenery get from the workshop to the stage? Is there a maximum dimension for any one piece?

PREPARING A GROUND PLAN

A CASE STUDY

Your ground plan is a diagrammatic aerial view of the setting. Eventually you will have to produce a more precise technical drawing (line drawing), which will be a major source of information for the whole production team.

Start with a series of very small rough drawings. Do not worry much about scale but try to find a place for everything and indicate it simply. You will find your designer's grid useful here. It will remind you of what you have identified as necessary and help you not to miss important points.

As your ideas get more refined, you will want to work to scale to ensure that your decisions are physically feasible. At this stage it is best to work on tracing paper over your

theatre ground plan. This lets you check sightlines more precisely.

THE FINISHED GROUND PLAN

Your finished ground plan must be detailed and accurate and include all the information an overhead diagram can convey. Note, on this ground plan, the following details:

■ the inclusion of centre and setting lines,
■ the varying thicknesses of lines for extra clarity
■ the use of labels where information cannot be conveyed visually
■ the indication of levels, including written heights
■ the information box.

You may also like to check the ground plan for sightlines, for naturalness of furniture positions and variety of acting areas.

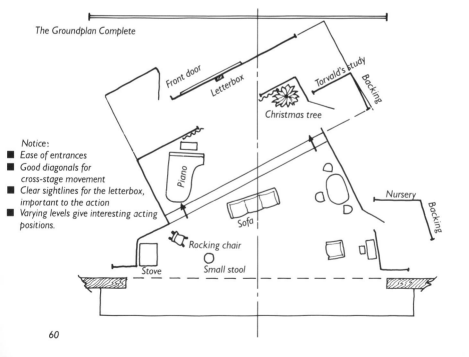

The Groundplan Complete

Front door Letterbox Torvald's study Backing Christmas tree

Notice:
■ Ease of entrances
■ Good diagonals for cross-stage movement
■ Clear sightlines for the letterbox, important to the action
■ Varying levels give interesting acting positions.

Piano Nursery Backing Sofa Rocking chair Stove Small stool

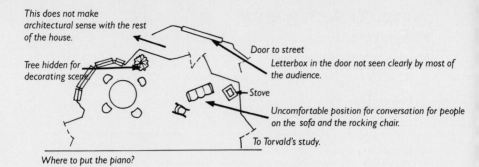

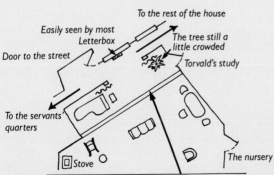

MAKING A SKETCH FROM A GROUND PLAN

Before arriving at a finished design you may want to sketch what you propose, a useful way to show your director a preliminary idea and a means of trying out suggestions before making a full-scale model. You can also use a sketch to prepare colour ideas or to indicate to the lighting designer how you imagine a scene being lit.

There are some dangers in presenting ideas via a drawing. You may distort the relative sizes of scenery to emphasize the dramatic effect you have in mind, giving a false impression of what space is available and exactly what the ground plan implies.

You can get a relatively accurate idea of the sizes and relationships of areas by basing a scenic sketch on your ground plan. The method outlined here is quick and easy, and it will give you a fairly accurate result because most stages are not deep, and so perspective distortions will be minimal.

Centre the ground plan below your drawing paper, the setting line parallel to the bottom of the paper. With straight edge and set square draw vertical lines to indicate the positions of important points – the edges of flats, corners of furniture and so on.

Indicate the proscenium arch at either side, making it correct scale height. You can then divide this into various measurement divisions from which to calculate all the heights on the sketch.

Provide yourself with a horizon line, using pins and cotton, extending it on either side beyond the drawing. It should be placed at the scale equivalent of an average eye level, for instance three inches above your setting line if you are using scale 1:24. You can work to a central vanishing point on this line. Other vanishing points you need can be marked anywhere on the thread.

You should now be able to use the simple perspective rules on page 72 to draw your sketch. It will be greatly enhanced if you use a simple colour wash to add light and shade for emphasis. Anyway, you can be confident that, being based on the scale ground plan, it quite accurately represents your intent.

Preparing a sketch from your groundplan

CHAPTER 5

FROM GROUND PLAN TO DESIGN

In moving from ground plan to completed design you will have to establish the visual style of your setting. This is important because it will fundamentally affect the kind of decisions you must take. Different styles make diferent demands on designers.

Choose the visual style that you judge will best bring out the mood of the play. Would it be funnier – or more poignant – if the audience believed the situation before them to be a real event? If you judge so then *Realism* is the style for your play.

Does the play discuss universal ideas that are not specific to one historical period? An *Abstract* style will help the audience to examine these ideas beyond a single social context.

If a play is based in reality but uses exaggeration for its dramatic or comic effect *Neo-Realism* is suggested.

Whichever style you adopt will present practical design considerations.

REALISM

Realism aims for an almost photographic copy of real life. Historical and social accuracy are essential, so you will need to do much detailed research.

In a realistic setting you are reproducing the everyday. It is a very immediate style, drawing the audience quickly into the picture. It also heightens the separation of spectators from stage; the actors cannot acknowledge the audience's existence. As a designer you may wish to reinforce this by, say, turning the backs of furniture to the audience.

Notes for a realistic design

Scale is very important in realism. Too large a space will make convincing furniture arrangements difficult. Try to use an area appropriate for the room you are creating.

■ the architectural features of the set should be very detailed and, where possible, three-dimensional
■ furniture arrangements are important. They must seem logical and uncontrived.
■ backings and views through windows need particular care and plenty of detail
■ choose real materials rather than imitations where possible. Any copies you use must be convincingly accurate
■ hire or find, rather than make, props
■ stage effects must be as close to the real thing as possible – e.g. real water to convey the impression of rain outside a window.

ABSTRACT DESIGN

This is for plays dealing with large concepts. It is design by suggestion and implication, using moods and intangible effects to create the environment, and suggesting a milieu through colour, shape and texture. The style calls on the designer to observe, synthesize and reinterpret. Its aim is poetic effect and it is best for plays that do not deal with the minutiae of life.

■ The design emphasis is on large, shared concepts. You may well wish to accentuate this by blurring the distinction between the audience's world and the actors'. You could, for example, build scenic elements out into the auditorium or bring your design forward on to the forestage, devices that will emphasize the universality of the play.

Notes for abstract design

■ use images that tap a universal response and are not too personal
■ vary the scale of the areas available to the cast. While creating a vast abstract space you must also cater for intimate scenes
■ you will have to find abstract alternatives for some things like doors and chairs
■ the props will probably all have to be designed, not found
■ effects may need designing in abstract terms, for instance silk fabric or light repre senting water.

NEO-REALISM

This style is for plays based in reality but which venture into the wilder regions of experience, such as comedies that start in the everyday but run to extraordinary situations. It also suits plays with conventional beginnings but contrived endings. Your design should have recognizably realistic origins but with an aspect stressed or exaggerated for comic or dramatic effect.

The style revels in theatricality and in acknowledging the audience's existence.

You can develop this by heightening the artificial division between audience and actors, perhaps with an auditorium lit up as brightly as the stage, or the whole play performed behind a decorative false proscenium.

Notes for neo-realism

■ the starting point for your design must be in a recognizable reality
■ the exaggerations should be authentic developments, however wild, from that base
■ your props will be both real and made objects, and when designed they will often be made from bits and pieces of real objects
■ you will face hard decisions about how far to push exaggerations and when to stick to reality. Whether an effect is real or exaggerated must not depend just on technical convenience.

Your choice of approach will of course be shared with your director. Be aware that it will affect more than the design. Your visual contributions must harmonize with what happens elsewhere in the production. Everyone involved must understand and follow the chosen style.

It is very important to be consistent. Audiences quickly accept any style but are puzzled when faced with an effect that is outside the original convention. However momentary a lapse, it asks them to re-evaluate the play's dramatic terms.

These three pictures show one designer's interpretation of realistic, neo-realistic and abstract design.

HISTORICAL RESEARCH

Applying correct historical data greatly enhances the credibility of a setting, but researching a particular period calls for time and resourcefulness.

■ research the period in depth, finding out about many aspects of its culture, not just its architecture but its social conventions, habits and the everyday things people used – furniture, fabrics, pottery, glassware, tools and transport
■ always seek primary sources – paintings, antiques, buildings – *in situ* or through photographs. Avoid copies or redrawn evidence; they may tell you more about the artists' prejudices than the real objects
■ seek underlying causes, such as the economic and social reasons for a fashion. Trade links, gluts or scarcities of materials, scientific discoveries, religious symbolism and other factors may lie at its roots and help you get to the heart of any style
■ from this understanding synthesize your detail. Do not simply copy the decorative elements; that will make your design seem naive
■ research alertly and creatively. The image you need may be in the carving on a chair back or on the sculpted base of a medieval font.

HOW TO RESEARCH A PERIOD

Decide just what period you must research and, even if it is obvious from the play (it may not be) broaden the dates involved. Go farther back at least twenty years – older people retain old tastes and habits – then forward five years to see what new ideas would have been stirring.

List the famous painters, architects, sculptors and craftsmen of the period. If you are unsure who they might be look up portraits of famous contemporaries and start with the artists who painted them. You will pick up a trail from there.

Use your library. You will find relevant information under Art, Architecture, Textiles, Social Science, History and Geography. Look for unusual sources of information – exhibition catalogues, mail order catalogues, family photo albums, old newspapers. Information will often lurk in the *background* of a painting or photograph, so look beyond the main subject.

USING HISTORICAL EVIDENCE

When you apply historical information to a setting for design purposes you *select* the details.

Use architectural detail for its personality as well as period accuracy. Choose a particular doorway because it expresses strength or a decoration for its florid character. Prefer a fabric for its elegance – or for its threadbare quality.

You may have to adapt the real thing by exaggerating features with the appropriate personality and cutting out inexpressive ones. A mass of unedited, slavishly-copied historical accuracies will be flavourless.

THE DESIGNER'S TOOLS – COLOUR

Colour is a valuable design tool and can heighten the mood and atmosphere of your settings. Your colour choices will largely be determined by observation and taste but you can learn to use simple rules and devices like the colour wheel given here. You might like to reproduce it in paint as a way of learning its simple rules.

THE COLOUR WHEEL

The wheel displays the elementary colours that make up white light. You can see several interesting and useful effects.

Each colour is a mixture of the other two.

Red, yellow and blue pigments are the primary colours from which all the others are made. They are less interesting than the secondary colours produced by mixing them. Still more complex and subtle hues can be achieved by blending secondaries with each other.

Segments near each other on the wheel offer naturally pleasing schemes. Exploit this by choosing one or two adjacent segments and picking your colours from within them. Add colours from other parts of the wheel only for sudden dramatic interest.

Colours fall into two groups: 'warm' – red, orange and the adjacent yellow – and 'cold'

– blue, adjacent greens and purples. These are useful properties for a designer creating an atmospheric mood.

Some colours have a very subtle 'temperature', being midway between obviously hot and cool hues. You can exploit this subtlety.

Each segment mirrors an opposing one on the wheel. These pairs are called 'complementaries' and when used adjacently they produce a vibrantly contrasting effect. If mixed together they produce a grey, and to add a little of one to the other is an interesting way of toning the colour down.

Adding white makes a colour appear less close, a useful effect for distancing an object. Adding black makes a colour less eye catching but still dramatic. It can be used to shift focus from one area to another

PREPARING A COLOUR SCHEME

If you find it hard to devise a colour scheme for your design, use pictures and other found objects to help you. A postcard reproduction, a patterned piece of cloth or a delicately coloured pebble or shell will suggest many shades and tones. Choose them for more than their attractive qualities. Every colour combination has a different effect. You are trying to recognize and exploit it to enhance your visual drama

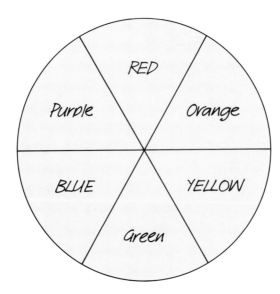

A colour wheel

USING TEXTURE

Textures can add depth and character to a setting. When you design naturalistically your scenery will seem more solid and 'real' if you recreate the buildings' surface qualities. Abstract settings can exploit the feelings that various materials evoke, using them instead of pictorial images to create a location's atmosphere.

Textured surfaces catch light in interesting ways, heightening the three-dimensional effect of modern stage lighting with dramatic shadows and highlights.

There are many alternatives to plain painted surfaces. Learn to exploit them by thinking in contrasts:

■ metallic surfaces can be impersonal – like cold grey iron – or warm – like glowing beaten-gold

■ corrosion adds a second quality to the hard shine of burnished steel

■ fur fabric can be sleek and sensual or long haired and primitive

■ wooden surfaces can be highly polished and impersonal or bleached pure by sea and sun

Use interesting materials for your model – marquetry woods for floors, old linoleum for rough roadways, coloured towelling for grass. Once you start realizing your design you must decide if you can use real materials for the scenery. They may be too expensive, heavy or out of scale, and you will have to find substitutes that recreate the qualities of the model. Meeting this challenge can be very rewarding, for texture evokes location in a most immediate way.

Using texture to evoke a location

69

ENHANCING THE GROUND PLAN

CREATING ATMOSPHERE WITH SHAPES

Shapes can communicate feelings and moods just as colours and textures can. Use them to enhance the atmosphere of your setting. Though you are accurately reproducing a period style you will heighten the effect by carefully choosing the shapes within it.

Sometimes the script will suggest shapes to use. You may feel, for example, that a scene is warm and generous, needing soft rounded outlines. For a coldly analytical atmosphere you will be thinking of appropriate angular shapes.

Another way is to start from the characters, using their environment to reflect their personalities. You might emphasize the raucous bonhomie of a drinking circle by using only rounded furniture, plump circular cushions and bellied cups and jugs. Meanness could be conveyed by making all his household implements narrow and thin. The idea could be taken all over the design with a spiky top for his front door and windows with narrow elongated panes.

Notice that these examples concern abstract qualities: thinness, roundness, meanness. They are suggested for their inherent 'personalities'. Try to think in this way so that shapes you adopt are not just similes. If you think and select in purely abstract terms you can apply the technique throughout your setting.

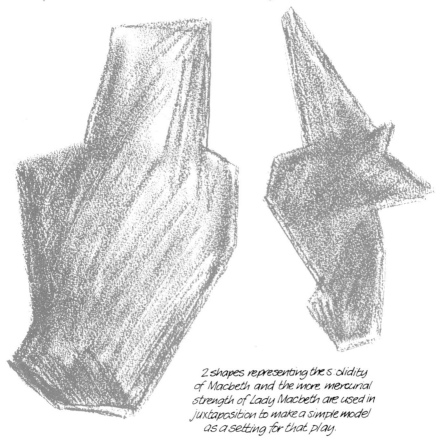

2 shapes representing the solidity of Macbeth and the more mercurial strength of Lady Macbeth are used in juxtaposition to make a simple model as a setting for that play.

USEFUL GEOMETRICAL CONSTRUCTIONS

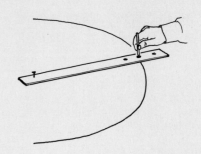

Drawing a circle

Use a simple compass made from a piece of string and a nail. For a more accurate circle use a piece of wood with a hole drilled in it for your pencil or chalk.

Drawing an ellipse

Mark the horizontal and vertical axes of your ellipse. Put two nails at the points on the horizontal axis described by the length of the vertical axis. Tie a piece of string the length of the horizontal axis to the nails. With your pencil or chalk inside the string draw the perfect ellipse that the string stretches to.

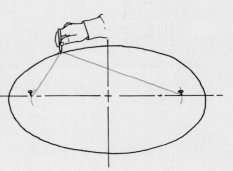

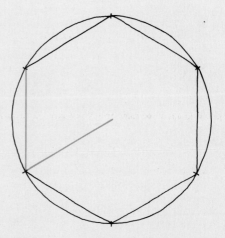

Drawing a hexagon

Draw a circle. Use a compass to divide the circumference into six lengths equal to the *radius* of the circle. Join up these points for a perfect hexagon.

PERSPECTIVE, A VALUABLE TOOL

You will sometimes want to create an illusion of great depth on stage. This can be done with false perspective.

The eye judges distance by indications like the spaces between verticals and the apparent slope of horizontals. Parallel lines seem closer together the further off they are. Using these simple rules you can make viewers think that your sets are larger or deeper than they are.

If you use perspective you should remember some basic points:

■ stage perspective relies on one central viewing point and is most suited to a proscenium theatre, not theatre in the round nor most thrust stages
■ the wider the stage the less easy it is to use this kind of visual trick. From the outer seats the perspective lines will be seen as mere distortion
■ actors cannot become smaller as they go down a false perspective. Use the effect carefully, where you know they will not have to act, and estimate how they will look

■ doors and windows in perspective will have sloping horizontals. This can make for odd visual effects as they open and practical difficulties if they swing upstage on a slope
■ you can add to your effect by emphasizing distance with colour. Things farther away appear lighter in tone.

The following drawings describe a simple perspective method using an horizon as an eye level and making lines converge on a vanishing point.

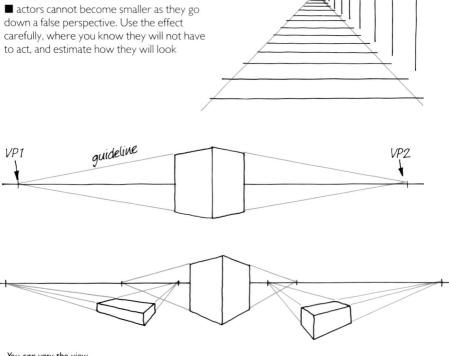

You can vary the view you choose by altering the horizon/eye level and the vanishing point.

Here is a useful method of marking out a floor using perspective to give it added depth. Count the number of tiles to a width. Divide the horizontal nearest you (A) into equal parts.

Draw lines from these division points towards the vanishing point. Then judge visually the depth of a square into which you can fit, say, three lines per side. Draw this square into one of the angles as shown (lines B & C).

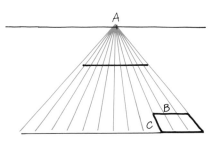

Draw a diagonal to cut this square into two through vertices D and B, giving you points E, F, G, H and so on.

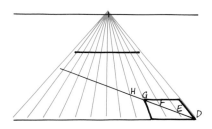

You can now place the horizontals to make up the pattern. When all the points are fixed, draw in the next diagonal, always make the square three tiles per side until the pattern is completed.

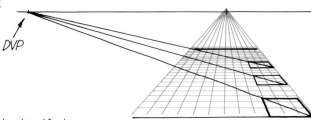

The above technique can be adapted for the division of a space into equal parts. Here again it is a double operation. The measuring point is placed half-way up the vertical nearest us. The ground line is extended on both sides of that vertical division of each of the two planes as shown.

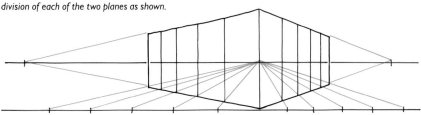

GROUND PLAN INTO MODEL

To translate the bare bones of your ground plan into a finished model set you need a variety of ideas. They can have many sources. The model for *A Doll's House* will enhance the formal precision of the ground plan with design features that place it historically, add atmosphere through colour and texture, and use form in an interesting abstract way.

Historical research
Ideas for furniture can be found in illustrated exhibition catalogues, paintings of the period and museums. A chair back may even inspire the nature of the wallpaper to be chosen. Architectural detail will be important and chosen for its evocative accuracy.

Textures
Various materials will be considered to give the right textural qualities for the scene. Some marquetry veneers used on the model could eventually be matched with stained and varnished wood on the finished setting.

Colour scheme
Postcard reproductions of Norwegian architecture are to be looked at for a colour scheme, but the hues in a piece of fabric may suggest the right atmosphere.

MAKING A MODEL BOX

Your model must be an exact scale replica of your stage. Only in this way can you judge the design's proportions properly. Take great care in making your model box. It should be strongly constructed and as detailed as is practicable. Plan carefully before you start; think out exactly what you feel you must reproduce.

Make a solid base board; 12 mm (1/2 in) plywood is ideal. You can cut your walls from thick card or Kappa board – a foam-cored paper – and glue them directly to the base board. Use black card if you can get it; otherwise paint it a matt black.

The box should be three or four inches higher than your proscenium opening. Judge which of the theatre's walls you must reproduce. They will usually be the darkest lines on your ground plan. Work to their on-stage edge but model the thickness of the proscenium arch. With a thrust stage or theatre in the round you may feel that you must also model the surrounding steps and vomitories. You will also have to include wing space but not storage.

Inner-proscenium arches, teasers (tormentors) and legs can be modelled in a thinner mounting card and glued into place. Borders should also be made of this material and hung from a length of half-inch-square balsa wood glued along their top edges.

Cloths and gauzes (scrims)

Like borders, cloths should be made from white mounting card and hung from the edge of your model box by balsa wood glued to their tops. Gauzes (scrims) are more difficult. If they have a design on them model them as a cloth. Vision gauzes for a misting effect can be simulated with nylon net or aluminium mesh.

A simple flying system

Fix the positions of flown cloths and borders with pins in the top edges of your theatre's walls. By this means balsa wood supports can be aligned exactly with the ground plan positions

Pins in horizontal cross-pieces over the stage are the basis of any flying effect you may need. Glue button thread to your model

pieces as hanging lines. Small safety pins tied to the ends of the cotton can be hooked over dressmaker's pins in the side of the box, allowing you to reproduce different flying positions and heights.

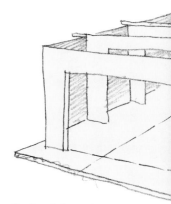

Cardboard wings and borders are added as one piece

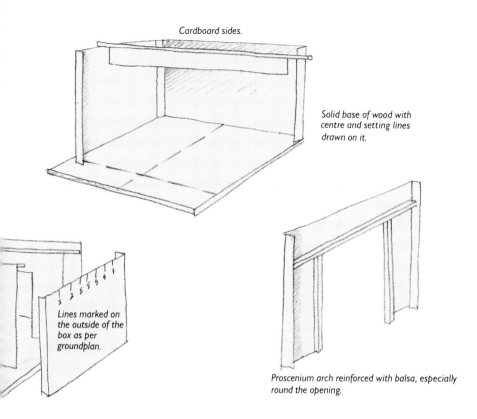

Cardboard sides.

Solid base of wood with centre and setting lines drawn on it.

Lines marked on the outside of the box as per groundplan.

Proscenium arch reinforced with balsa, especially round the opening.

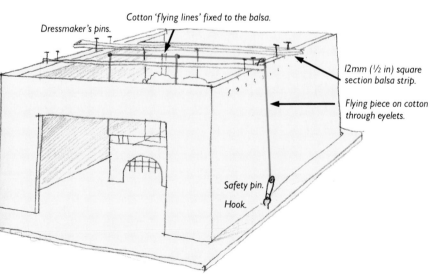

Dressmaker's pins.

Cotton 'flying lines' fixed to the balsa.

12mm (½ in) square section balsa strip.

Flying piece on cotton through eyelets.

Safety pin.

Hook.

CHAPTER 6

MODEL MAKING

You will model your set to scale from your ground plan and sketch model, using mainly six-sheet white card. Now is the time for firm decisions about the height and shape of elevations. You can draw a whole room, its walls joined edge-to-edge, then fold them into position. The tops and sides of rostra (platforms) and steps are drawn separately and glued together. Details like windows and doors must be designed fully now and drawn in place.

Cut out what you have drawn to scale on the card. Use a very sharp knife for an accurate finish; scissors produce rough, curled edges. Cut against a steel straight edge, not your scale ruler; you will ruin its technical precision.

Use a wooden cutting board to preserve your blades and protect the table top, and keep your fingers safely behind the blade when cutting.

To bend the card first score it – half cut through it – remembering that the card bends *away* from the scored edge. This lets you, for instance, model a door hinged to open either way. By scoring alternately on two sides of a strip of card, you can produce the treads and risers of a flight of steps, then fold them into place on two neatly cut sides.

With contact adhesive – apply a little to *both* surfaces and wait a few minutes – you can stick pieces together instantly, and not have to hold them in place until fixed.

BASIC TOOL KIT

You will need:

- a ruler with either a 1:24 or 1:25 scale
- a metal straight edge for cutting against
- a set square
- a pair of pencil compasses
- a sharp hard pencil

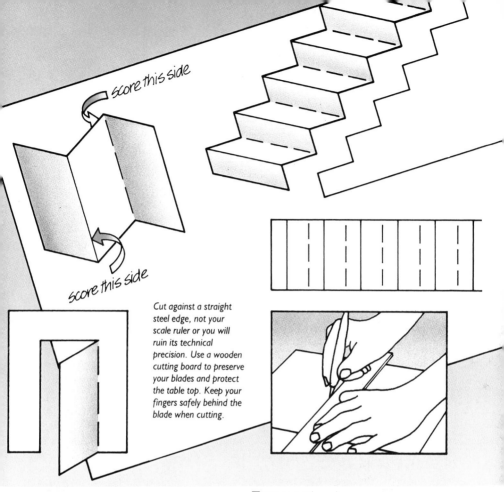

score this side

score this side

Cut against a straight steel edge, not your scale ruler or you will ruin its technical precision. Use a wooden cutting board to preserve your blades and protect the table top. Keep your fingers safely behind the blade when cutting.

■ paper-cutting scissors
■ a sharp modelling knife with either a 'snap-off' or replaceable blade
■ a softwood cutting board
■ model makers' contact adhesive such as Bostik No. 1 or Scotch contact adhesive

You may also want:

■ various adhesive tapes
■ gouache paints and paint brushes
■ spray paints
■ fine modelling clay such as Meilliput.

Working to scale

Working with a scale ruler helps you to get exact measurements easily and quickly. Note the difference between reading a metric rule and an imperial one.

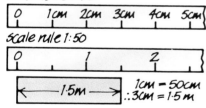

Centimetre rule

| 0 | 1CM | 2CM | 3CM | 4CM | 5CM |

Scale rule 1:50

| 0 | 1 | 2 |

← 1·5m →

1CM = 50CM
∴ 3CM = 1·5 m

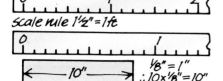

Inch rule

| 0 | 1″ | 2″ |

Scale rule 1½″ = 1ft

| 0 | 1 |

← 10″ →

⅛″ = 1″
∴ 10 x ⅛″ = 10″

MORE MODEL MAKING

Using balsa wood

Add detail to your basic card model with balsa wood. It is sold in many different sizes and cross sections and can be glued on for door frames, mouldings, baseboards and covings; also used to make fireplaces, balustrades and furniture.

You can carve this soft wood with your knife or shape it with sandpaper, and it is easily glued together with the contact adhesive.

Textures

Gluing various materials to a model will produce pleasing results, and a search for interesting imitation finishes to use will be well worthwhile.

- cut thin sheet balsa into floorboard sizes, then stain and varnish it as you wish
- bring lively surfaces of metallic or patterned papers into your design
- use sheets of clear acrylic plastic as a substitute for glass.

You may have to produce your own textures by, say, cutting card into flagstones or bricks and sticking them on. Drinking straws will suggest other effects and so will various fabrics. Keep your eyes open for unusual things to use and build up a collection of the most promising ones.

Fabrics and draperies.

On a scale model it is almost impossible to use real fabrics as drapery. They are not flexible enough to be convincing and must be represented in other ways. You can use plaster bandage dipped in water and set into permanent swathes for curtains, bedclothes, etc. You can draw the effect you want on flat card or build up an imitation cloth with tissue paper dipped in paste.

Trees and foliage

These too are hard to reproduce to scale. Model makers' sphagnum moss dyed appropriately is one easy answer, and you can also adapt plastic ferns and other plants. But you may have to carve foliage from balsa blocks or building up trees with plaster bandage or tissue paper on twigs.

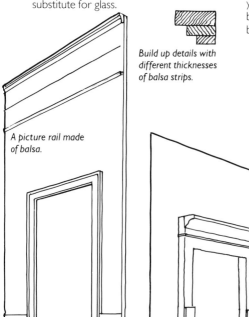

Build up details with different thicknesses of balsa strips.

A picture rail made of balsa.

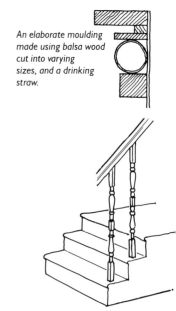

An elaborate moulding made using balsa wood cut into varying sizes, and a drinking straw.

Carved balsa strip for balustrades.

Using balsa to build up model details.

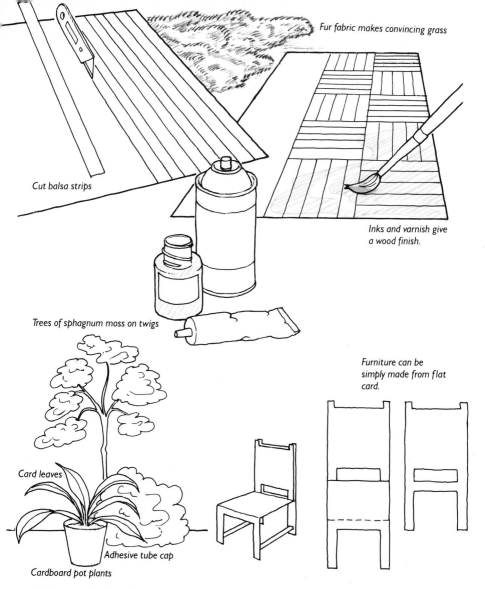

Fur fabric makes convincing grass

Cut balsa strips

Inks and varnish give a wood finish.

Trees of sphagnum moss on twigs

Furniture can be simply made from flat card.

Card leaves

Adhesive tube cap

Cardboard pot plants

Making model furniture

Furniture on your model set can show the director and actors its disposition and personality. If it is sufficiently well done it will communicate a lot to them and to the craftsmen who will have to find the real thing or realize it. Remember – you are working to scale and it must be the right size.

Most furniture will be cut from card, with balsa additions, but you can build up details by assembling tiny found objects. By gluing together small washers, beads, springs, sprockets and screws you can model such intricate things as ornate carved legs for a chair or table. They will also make table lamps, plates and trays. You can use a glue-gun to blob detail on to the basic wood and card shapes, and your modelling clay can be rolled into a long sausage, shaped and baked dry. Sometimes you can use things like jewellery mounts for picture frames and cake decorations for chandeliers.

STARTING TO MAKE A MODEL – RIDERS TO THE SEA

Get a quick idea of what three-dimensional forms your ground plan suggests and with scissors and card make a very rough sketch model, securing it with masking tape and glue. You will soon spot ideas that do not translate quite as you had imagined and will be able to correct them before laboriously making a proper model. Gradually, as you decide what is right, you will work more accurately.

The designer of this model corrects an unfortunately placed entrance in the original quick card sketch. As detail is added to the design other corrections create a more pleasing arrangement of the abstract leaf shapes.

You may need several such stages before you are ready to make a well-defined model. Use modelling as a thinking process; try to respond to *what you see*. Often a good visual idea will emerge by accident, and you must be able to recognize and use it. For example the unplanned inclusion of some vertical twigs has a happy result. It breaks up the acting area and provides an alternative for the bower and a hiding place.

The final ground plan may have to be ad-justed to take account of any new ideas. It can be prepared only when model-making is completed.

PAINTING AND PRESENTATION

Your finished model must be carefully painted and presented in a model box so that your director gets as accurate an impression as possible. You are selling him your ideas, so they must be shown to best advantage.

Remember that you can emphasize your effects and give focus to your design with painted light, directing the viewer's eye to the acting areas by making them lighter or by adding painted shadow to the outer edges of your stage.

When painting white card it is best to start with light background colours and paint darker shadows on to them. Each time you apply a colour dry the surface with an absorbent paper towel. In this way you can control the paint and not reach an irremovable dark tone too quickly.

Spray paints are useful for adding a general shadow but difficult to use accurately, so you should practise before using them on a valuable model.

A quick card sketch is roughly cut out using scissors and taped together.

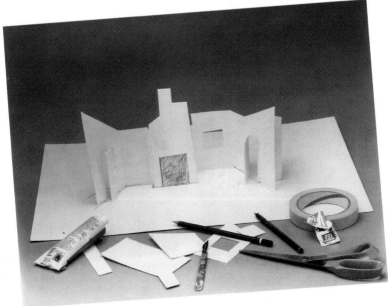

Doors and windows are repositioned. A ceiling is added and the fireplace redesigned. Detail is gradually built up.

The completed model, painted and presented in the model box is an exact representation of the designer's intention.

PREPARING TECHNICAL (LINE) DRAWINGS

The purpose of drawings

The workshop staff will need more than the scale model to work from, and exact technical (line) drawings will give them answers to questions during the building process when you are not around. Dimensions and shapes of many details will be obscured in the model and you must communicate those and other information in precise diagrammatic manner.

Even if you are to construct the scenery yourself you must make careful drawings before starting. Preparing them will help you to foresee many difficulties and have a plan of action, with measurements and processes, already clearly established.

Remember – time spent at the drawing board is time saved in the workshop.

What to communicate

The examples given here show how you might lay out technical drawings.

A check list of requirements is helpful:

■ does the information box give details of the production's name, venue, director and designer, and – very important – the scale of the drawings? Where more than one sheet of drawings is prepared they should be numbered – e.g. '1 of 12 '.

■ is every dimension clearly marked? When a size can be decided only in construction it should be noted

■ verbal information should be precise and neatly written in note form

■ when a particular material is required be sure that the covering is specified

■ open spaces must be marked

■ fine detail of mouldings or intricate construction may have to be drawn to a different scale. Indicate this *very* clearly and show the exact position of the detail

■ label the pieces of scenery individually. You may have to number them according to a ground plan scheme

■ for extra clarity use varying thicknesses of line in your drawing

■ have you done a drawing for *every* piece of scenery?

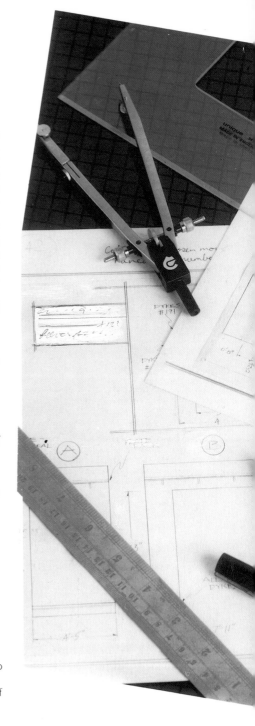

CHAPTER 7

WORKSHOP TECHNIQUES

SCENE-BUILDING – TOOLS AND METHODS

You need only minimal equipment to build scenery; most jobs can be done with the tools listed below. Sometimes, for touring or for especially complicated settings, more complex techniques are necessary, but that is unusual. The sophisticated equipment in a professional scene shop is mainly for speeding up the building process.

A tool kit for scene-building

■ power jig-saw
■ power-drill with various bits, including 25 mm (1in) and 12 mm (½in) spade bits
■ rip saw
■ tenon saw
■ ratchet screwdriver
■ claw hammer
■ set of chisels
■ staple gun
■ carpenter's set square
■ wood rasp
■ sharp craft knife
■ steel tape measure
■ PVA wood adhesive

MAKING A SIMPLE FLAT

The basic frame is made from 75 × 25 mm (3 × 1in) wood with horizontal stretchers every 90 cm (3 feet) to keep it square.

The simplest method employs butt joints braced with triangles of 9 mm (3/8 in) plywood screwed (or nailed) and glued with PVA. A more solid flat can have half-lap and

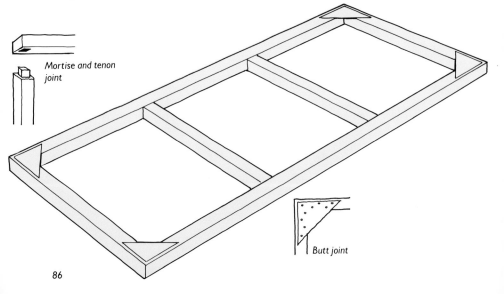

Mortise and tenon joint

Butt joint

screwed joints, and mortise-and-tenon joints give door flats greater strength.

Do not forget to drill the hole for your cleat line and add the cleat hook before canvassing.

CANVASSING

When you attach the canvas to the flat fix your first fastenings to the centre of each rail and work outwards, going from side to side to stretch the canvas fairly tightly. Remember that it will shrink when painted.

Canvas can be simply wrapped round the wooden frame and stapled to the back, but for a professional finish tack the cloth temporarily to the inner faces of the rails, then apply hot carpenter's glue to the undersurface and smooth the canvas down with a hot damp cloth. Brisk rubbing foams the glue through the material and ensures a secure finish. Cut away excess canvas with your knife and finally remove the tacking nails.

Flats can be covered with hardboard or plywood if a particular finish needs a rigid surface – or to prevent shaking, by an adjacent door for instance.

Making a simple flat

Cut glued down canvas with knife.

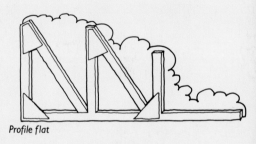

Canvassing

Profile Flats

Frames for these are made in the same way as those for rectangular flats but with extensions for the outer shapes. Be sure to have enough support for the profile edge by cutting out the shape first and building the frame on top of it. Profile flats are covered with plywood or hardboard, so you must provide a fixing where the covering materials' edges join.

For uniform surface texture the whole flat should be covered with glued-on canvas, so you can cut away sections of the hardboard under the cloth to lighten the flat for scene shifting.

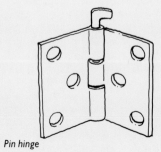

Profile flat

Pin hinges

These are useful devices for fixing scenery temporarily, either edge to edge or to a predetermined position on the stage. The pin, attached with string to the hinge so as not to get lost, is quickly removed during a scene change. Pin hinges can be bought from ironmongers or hardware stores, or made by grinding out the centre pins of backflap hinges. Nails can be used as substitute pins.

Pin hinge

THREE-DIMENSIONAL SCENERY

RIGID PLATFORMS

Constructing rigid platforms is relatively easy. They are more quickly built and are less expensive than the folding type. You can use them if you have no storage problems or if your rostra (parallels) are to be permanently set throughout the performance. The diagram shows how you can use simple carpentry with strap-iron corners instead of complicated joints. On various occasions the tops can be used with legs of different heights, but if they are more than a foot high they will need the bracing shown in the drawing.

The sides of your rostrum will have to be faced with hardboard and the tops probably padded for soundproofing.

FOLDING PLATFORMS

These useful stock items require half-lap or mortise-and-tenon joints to make their four sides strong enough. Their hinging pattern is complicated, as the drawing shows, but it allows the platforms to be stored in very little space.

The top is made from three-quarter-inch plywood or blockboard stiffened with 100 x 25mm/4 x 1in battening, which also fixes the lid in place.

DOOR AND WINDOW FLATS

You will probably want to build a 'dependent' doorway, one fixed permanently to its flat. The diagram shows the various construction points. Check at all times that the door itself and the framing round it are square, .

When hanging the door in the frame stand it on a piece of hardboard to ensure that it clears the ground easily when it swings open. A window is made in the same way and can have stiles down to the ground behind the flat to bear the weight of the reveals.

An 'independent' door is made to fit in the space fixed by its surrounding architrave and can thus be saved and used in several different flats. Note that it must have 'sill irons' at its base to keep it square.

SIMPLE TREADS

As the diagram shows, making stair treads is very like making model ones. If your steps are more than three feet wide you must use three stretchers to support them. The risers do not bear any weight and so can be made from plywood or hardboard.

A folding platform

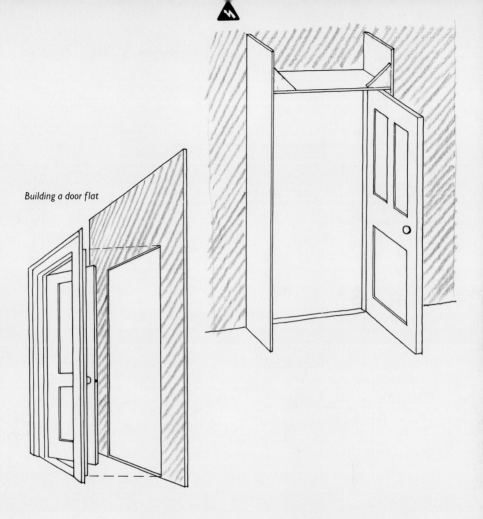

Building a door flat

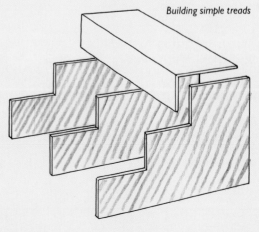

Building simple treads

VARIATIONS ON THREE-DIMENSIONAL SCENERY

Building a ramp
The diagram tells you that a ramp must be very strongly built. This one folds flat and would benefit from having mortise-and-tenon joints. Placing of the battens under the top is crucial; they prevent it slipping down the frame when in use. If the ramp is more than three feet wide you will need more centre support.

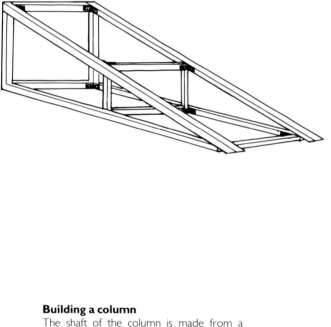

Building a column
The shaft of the column is made from a series of diminishing circles cut from block-board and notched to carry the two-by-one-inch vertical supports. The whole is covered with skin plywood or canvas and an elaborate capital can be made of felt, paper rope or papier mâché.

This construction is easily adapted to form a tree trunk. Cover it with chicken wire and glue-soaked canvas and add some branches.

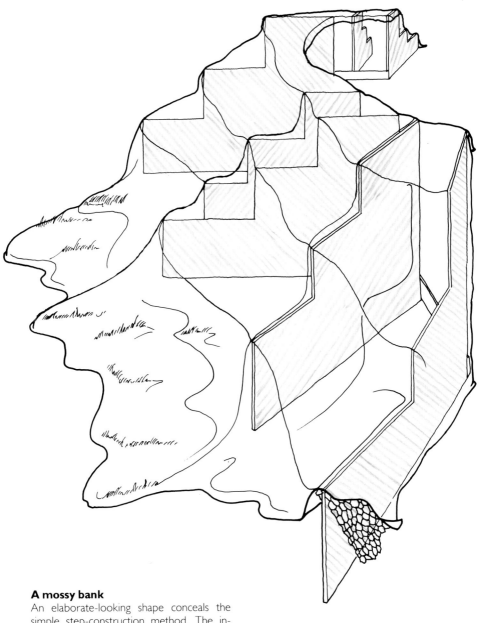

A mossy bank

An elaborate-looking shape conceals the simple step-construction method. The informal bank is built up like a geographical model, with 'practical' surfaces of three-quarter-inch blockboard and sides moulded from chicken wire. The whole is covered with glue-soaked canvas, then painted or finished with artificial grass, fun fur, or some other texture.

CHAPTER 8

SCENE PAINTING

Scene painting techniques are quite different from those of house-painting or easel-painting, but they can be acquired with practice. The paint used, its application and above all the scale of the work demand a particular style and method.

THE ART OF THE SCENE PAINTER

You need only minimal equipment to start. The hard part is finding working space, a large area where you can lay flats down or stretch out backcloths for painting. Your workshop must have a water supply and a sink with good drainage. It should also be warm and well ventilated; otherwise your scenery will dry slowly. Good ventilation is essential if using heavy-vapour paints.

The scene painter's varied job

■ you may have to paint large-scale visual illusions – landscapes or interiors – to persuade an audience that they are looking at something three dimensional
■ you may have to reproduce abstract drawings, simple graphic effects and areas of colour enlarged several times
■ you may be asked to counterfeit materials, to build up textured surfaces as brick or marble, or to produce imitation leaves, grass or rocks.

Whatever is demanded, the great skill is to hide your method. Disguise brush strokes so that they are not obvious.

Scene painting equipment

Special brushes and other equipment for scene painting can be bought from theatrical suppliers, but you will find of your needs in art shops and domestic paint stores.

Brushes

You can paint very effectively with good-quality house-painting brushes. They will hold enough paint and will maintain their shape well enough.
Get some 15 cm (6 in) brushes for under-coating, 10 and 7.5 cm (4 and 3 in) ones for painting large areas, and 5 and 2.5 cm (2 and 1 in) ones for detailed work and lines.
Fitches and lining brushes are used for drawing in paint. Brushes with specially long handles are useful for painting on the floor but they can be improvised.

Other tools

You can use mohair or sponge paint rollers on large areas and achieve some unusual effects. Taped to broom handles they are especially helpful in painting floors.
A vital piece of equipment is a real sponge; an artificial one is no substitute. Buy the biggest you can find. It can be dipped in paint and dabbed on a surface for textured effects and to soften the colour beneath.
Have as many buckets and empty tins as possible to hold mixed paint and keep a supply of sticks for mixing and stirring.

Drawing equipment

For preliminary drawing you will need chalk and charcoal so that you can see your marks on different coloured backgrounds. Charcoal particularly is easy to dust off after painting is finished.

An expanding steel tape measure at least 3 metres/10 feet long and a metre or yard stick are essential for marking out.

Neat lines can be achieved by drawing your brush along a straight edge. Any piece of wood will do but one with a bevelled edge prevents paint accumulating underneath and causing smudging. A handle on your straight edge is especially useful; it can be extended for painting standing up, as shown.

Long chalk lines are marked out with a snap line, which you can improvise. You can also make yourself compass with a nail and string or a drilled piece of wood.

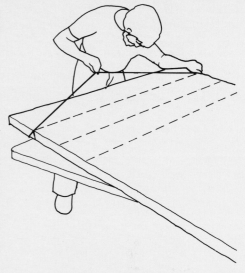

Spray guns

Many subtle effects can be achieved with a spray gun. Softening painted surfaces, adding areas of shadow and reaching difficult corners can all be done with an electric compressor spray. It must be carefully maintained to stay at peak performance but it is worth the trouble.

More easily obtained are hand-pumped plastic garden sprays (Hudson sprays) but they are harder to control. They are useful only for simple effects, like spraying over stencils and producing heavy blobbed textures.

Using a spray gun

Spray guns quickly block up with impurities and must be used only with filtered paint. Filter your paint through a double thickness of gauze or a nylon stocking into the cannister.

Clean the gun thoroughly the moment you have finished using it, taking special care with the nozzle components. Never leave the compressor running unnecessarily as that will dry out the paint in the gun's fine pipes.

You will need to practice using a spray gun. Spray from side to side in one smooth movement to prevent concentration of paint at either edge of the work. Remember – you are trying to disguise the method behind your scene painting.

SCENE PAINTING TECHNIQUES

PREPARING THE SURFACE

All component parts of a setting must be prepared in the same way so as to match when fitted together after painting. For this reason an undercoat called priming is the first thing painted on any scenery.
It has two effects:

■ all subsequent colours are applied over a uniform undercoat

■ the porous surface of the wood or canvas is filled in, ensuring that further paint does not sink into the materials.

The usual paint used for priming is cheap white emulsion. It can be quite thin, diluted with two parts of water. Some materials may need priming with different thicknesses of paint; for instance a backcloth for touring needs a very thin undercoat so that it can be folded without creasing.
If you paint with aniline dyes you need not prime the surface. They can be put directly on to the cloth.
Your priming has to be forced into the pores of the material. Apply vigorously, moving your brush in all directions. Start at the top of the flat and work down so that accidental dribbles will be neither wasteful nor uncorrected. Priming must be completely dry before the next coat of paint can be applied.

DRAWING UP THE DESIGN

Enlarging a drawing from a small sketch or model piece is quite simple. Fix a grid of squares, drawn on a transparent film, over the design. If you are working in the 1:24 scale half-inch squares will probably be appropriate. Where detail is very fine you may need a smaller pattern.
A matching grid of one-foot squares can be marked on the scenery as a guide. A few marks located on the small grid and copied on to the large one will provide you with a key. Complete the drawing using these as starting points. Try to be bold and draw freely. A tentative line looks constricted and unconvincing.

BRUSH TECHNIQUES

Taking care of your brushes
Brushes are expensive so you should take care of them, washing them out thoroughly after each use. Make sure that you get *all* the paint out of the 'heel' of the brush, where the bristles join the handle, by running water down into them. Keep a bucket of clean water by you when painting, and rinse brushes out and store them to prevent them drying hard.
A brush can be used to cover large areas and also to paint lines. Large areas are filled in with the multi-directional technique described for priming. Draw a narrow straight line by resting the brush against a straight edge and drawing it towards you with a single smooth stroke.

Wet blend
A plain first coat of colour is often made more interesting by blending together two or more shades. Using separate brushes and buckets of colour, paint fairly large adjacent areas and blend them together where they meet. You can merge them into each other while they are still wet but you may need a bucket of clean water as a supplement.

Dry brush
A useful textured effect can be had with 'dry brush' technique. It is very effective as shading or for adding painted metallic highlights. After being dipped in the paint the brush is emptied of most of the colour by shaking or wiping out. When it is dragged lightly over the scenery a hatched dry effect is produced.

Stippling
An interesting texture is made by dabbing paint on from the tips of the bristles with a fierce stabbing movement. Stippling can be used to break up a uniform surface and to force paint through a stencil.

Splatter

A painted surface can be made more interesting by flicking or shaking a patina of paint blobs over it from a full brush. It can be done with surprising control.

Several different colours applied like this give a shimmering effect to a plain or wet blended area.

Splattering white paint will soften and distance detailed painting. If a hue is splattered on its complementary it brightens the original colour by contrast.

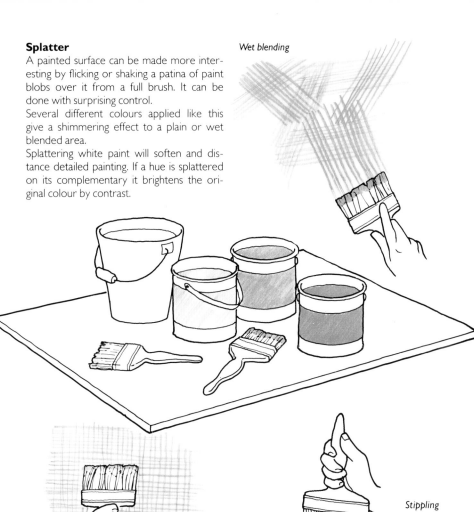

Wet blending

Dry brushing

Stippling

Splattering

PATTERNS AND TEXTURES

STENCILS

You may want to repeat a pattern on a setting – a wallpaper, a pillar capital, a fancy border. Stencilling is the best way of painting the same thing many times over.

A cut stencil

Cut your pattern with a very sharp knife from a strong and fairly waterproof material. Lampshade fabric is suitable; it can be cut into a fine pattern and its waxy surface means that it will not easily curl or disintegrate when wet.

Your design should be arranged so that it remains in one piece. If this is not possible the stencil can be stuck on to vision gauze to keep it together, though this material can make paint run under the pattern's edge unless you stipple very carefully.

Staple your stencil on to a wooden frame to keep the material stretched flat as you use it. Marks on the edge of the frame will help you to position it properly for repetition. With a good paintbrush stipple the paint through the cut pattern, holding the brush as vertically as you can. Some paint may bleed under the stencil, smudging your pattern, so keep checking and wiping off any excess.

A pounced pattern

To reproduce a *drawing* many times you can use a pounced pattern as a guide. Draw the design on strong brown paper and pierce holes through it along the lines, then 'pounce' powdered charcoal or graphite through the holes from a fine muslin bag on to the surface to be decorated.

A printing stencil

You can cut foam rubber into shapes to make printing stencils. Use a firm kind about two inches thick and glue the shape on to a stiff board. You can dip the stencil into a tray of paint or apply colour to the foam with a brush. This method is particularly useful for stencilling brickwork as the paint is sometimes unevenly applied.

Cut rollers

Foam rubber rollers can be cut with a knife or burned with a cigarette to make simple repetitive designs that are especially useful for linear or textured patterns. Remember to cut only halfway through the roller.

Combs

These can be used in various ways to make grained patterns on a painted surface.

String wrapped round the heel of a brush will separate the bristles to give a woodgrain effect.

Wooden or metal combs of various designs can be scraped through wet paint.

A small wooden roller with a carved surface can be used. Twist and turn it as you run it over the wet paint.

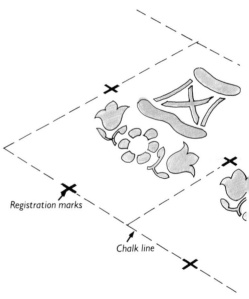

Registration marks

Chalk line

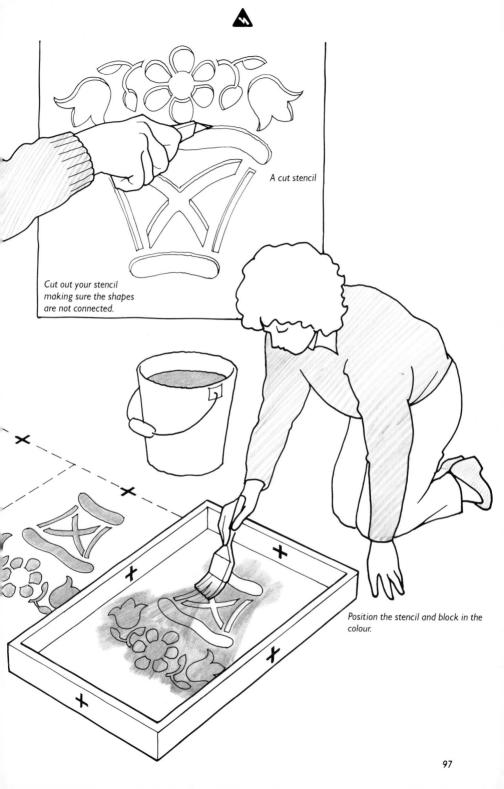

A cut stencil

Cut out your stencil
making sure the shapes
are not connected.

Position the stencil and block in the
colour.

PAINTING A BACKCLOTH

To paint a backcloth you need enough space to lay the whole cloth flat on the floor and walk round it. You must also have access to a water supply and sink. If you must keep the floor clean protect it with polythene sheeting.

The cotton in the backcloth will shrink when it is wet so you must counter that. If your floor is wooden and you can staple the cloth's edges to it; that is the ideal solution. If that is not possible you can place weights at two-foot intervals round the cloth's whole perimeter. Alternatively you can tack or staple the canvas temporarily to a wooden frame. Once the preliminary coats have dried and the cloth will not shrink any more you can remove all the fixings.

Use thin paint on the cloth, applying a series of coloured glazes to achieve your result.

When the white paint is dry use a snap line to draw a grid of squares on to the cloth. You can improvise the line by rubbing string with coloured chalk. Hold it taut on your measurement marks, raise it in the centre and snap the chalked line hard on the canvas.

The painting process should follow this order:

■ fill the weave with your priming coat
■ Cover most of the cloth with light background colours
■ add darker colours in the foreground
■ now do any detailed drawing, stencilling or painted textures. You should be using your darkest colours as you add hard edges for definition
■ finally paint bright highlights to emphasize the sculptural quality within your painting

With practice you will soon be able to sketch out the drawing needed in the larger scale from your original small sketch or model.

■ remember that during the process you can add splatter, spray, or other effect for softness, texture or distance.

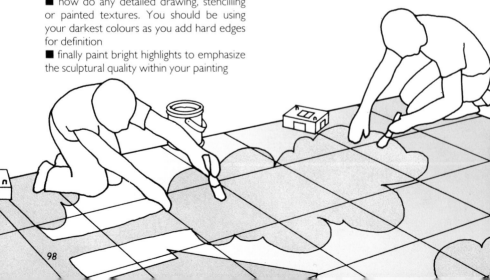

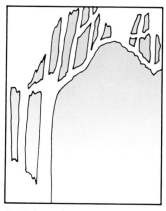

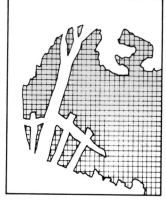

A well-designed cut cloth will need no extra support.

Here the lower part of the cloth needs supporting on the set to prevent it folding over.

PREPARING A CUT CLOTH

When cutting a painted cloth to shape you must remember that any parts not supported by hanging will flop and fall unconvincingly. There are a few ways round this:

■ you can glue a pocket of canvas behind the cloth. This would suit a feature such as a short branch sticking out from a tree trunk. The pocket should extend along the unsupported piece and into the body of the material. A dowel or light stick fitted down this as a cantilever will prevent the branch drooping

■ there is a special scenic netting for supporting complicated cut cloths. You align the 25mm (1in) cotton mesh both vertically and horizontally when laying it on the back of the cloth, then stipple latex adhesive on to it to fix it in place. When dry it supports the hanging cut cloth and any excess can be cut away.

■ a hole cut in a cloth can be filled with vision gauze (scrim) glued absolutely flat and taut on the back with latex adhesive

Variety is added to a cut cloth setting by cutting shapes and holes in the clothes. This adds depth to the scene, disclosing further distant views.

SPECIAL EFFECTS
APPLIED EFFECTS

Paper rope

This material can give very good decorative effects to scenery and properties. It may be had in several thicknesses from a half inch to three inches, and you can twist it into shapes on cornices, picture frames or furniture. Glue it in place with a hot-glue gun or any strong adhesive. To harden the rope saturate it in a stiffener such as PVA or glue size. It is bound in a fine net and will retain its shape, so it can be used even for relief sculpture.

Mirrors

Mirrors on stage can reflect glaring light into the audience's eyes. Spray them with a dulling substance like hair lacquer to overcome this. If your design demands a large mirror surface calculate its effect carefully.

You can use one of the special plastic mirror sheetings that are available. These must be stretched over a frame, glued or stapled into place and heated gently with a hair dryer to produce tension. Some mirror sheeting is thick enough to be stuck to a hardboard flat with contact adhesive. Use a very soft cloth to smooth or clean the mirrors as they are easily scratched.

Metallics

There is a wide choice of imitation metallic finishes. Fancy disco patterns, golds, silvers and anodized colours can all be bought in sheets and stuck on your scenery. They can be obtained from specialist suppliers like those listed in the glossary – and are quite expensive.

It can be hard to apply one of these to a flat that does not have a solid smooth face. Look for a *flexible* material, which will be easier to smooth – and remember to check that it conforms with fire safety standards.

Vacuum-formed scenery

A thin plastic sheeting can be formed by a vacuum-suction process into any decorative detail. Architectural decoration, brick patterns, columns, rows of book spines and many other useful pieces can be picked out of suppliers' catalogues and sent to you already shaped and ready for stapling on to your set. By grouping them skilfully you can get very ornate effects. They can be painted so as to be completely integrated into one surface. It is a time-saving – but fairly expensive – way of achieving an illusion of solidity. The forms are not strong, so they are not suitable for multiple scene changes or touring shows.

ULTRAVIOLET LIGHT

Ultraviolet light, often called 'black light', gives little illumination but will make special paints and fabrics glow dramatically in the dark. It works particularly well if over your ordinary scene painting you put a special transparent paint that is invisible until it is shown up in the dark by the ultraviolet light. With UV you could, for example, design an underwater sequence in which glowing images lit by it seem to float unsupported. The operators, in black costumes, are invisible against a dark surround.

PAINTED METAL EFFECTS

Gold, copper and silver paints are made from powders mixed with emulsion. Be sure to get the proportions right as too much emulsion makes the paint dull.

Use an undercoat colour as a base. Dark brown or yellow ochre is best for gold or copper, grey for silver. These preparatory coats will determine the effect of your metallic paint so choose them with care.

You can paint a shadow over the gold or silver finish with a thin emulsion glaze. Put a very small amount of base colour into a good quantity of dilute emulsion and paint it on top of the dried metallic surface. It will dry almost clear and leave the ochre or brown as a subtle shadow.

FRENCH ENAMEL VARNISH

FEV is a special varnish for painting on metal and other shiny surfaces. It is a mixture of shellac and dye and is diluted with methylated spirits. It is used for glazing shadows on pottery, armour, swords and so on.

GLITTER

Glitter dust gives an object a sparkling surface. It comes in gold, silver and other colours in varying grades of coarseness. Paint a clear emulsion glue over the area you want to sparkle, then sprinkle the glitter dust on top. Put paper under the work to collect any excess. The best results with this effect on a backcloth are got by lighting it from below by footlights. Be careful to apply glitter so that it cannot flake off and get on to actors' skins. It may cause irritating rashes or symptoms of hay fever.

CHAPTER 9

THE PRODUCTION WEEKEND

PREPARING FOR THE FIT-UP (PUT-IN)

In the few days before you move into your venue there are several things to be done:

■ attend final rehearsals to see that no problems have slipped by the consultation system

■ find out what schedule is being prepared for the fit-up (put-in) period so that you know when you must be available and if all potential difficulties have been foreseen. Make known any reservations you have about allocation of time and see that adjustments are made if possible

■ check that every prop has been found, hired or made. Most of the team will be busy, so expect no workshop time

■ make sure that painting is as advanced as can be and that time has been allowed for final touching up and floor painting on stage

■ take time to search through your lists, memory and intuition for any tiny problem that may still need solving. Such time will be well spent if it prevents a hold-up during the weekend.

AT THE FIT-UP (PUT-IN)

Whatever the size of your company you will be needed for several consultations at the fit-up (put-in). Your attention will be constantly in demand and you will need to be calm.

If you have a technical director make all your observations and requests through him. He is in charge of the whole stage team and can allocate work efficiently.

When you are your own stage supervisor think very carefully about the order in which jobs are to be done. Make sure that any working part of the set, any prop or furniture that actors must practise using or any painting that will greatly affect lighting are all finished in time for the technical rehearsal. Final painting and non-practical effects can be done at any time before the final dress rehearsal.

Follow your schedule and do not rush any judgements. You will be tempted to assess your work before it is complete. But scenery looks ugly under harsh working light, so wait until every part is in its place before commenting on construction and see it under theatrical lighting before assessing what further painting must be done.

You will have to give "deads" – final positions – on moving scenery, wagons, and flown pieces.

Watch for any misinterpretation of your intent as the setting is put together. You are available for guidance.

When a problem arises stay calm. First find out *exactly* what the difficulty is, then think of various solutions or ask the relevant technician for ideas. Estimate the consequences of any corrective action and plan your adjustment. *Do not be panicked into rash action*; the solution may be a simple one.

LIGHTING THE SET

Your role at the lighting sessions will be consultative, to help create the complete picture on stage. There are many things you may wish to comment on.

Watch what effect the tint of the light has on the scene painting. Check that it does not wash colour out or negate it.

Be aware of how shadows help or damage the sculptural qualities of your setting.

The lighting designer and the director will add light to dimly lit areas where acting will take place. You can help in this, having seen final dress rehearsals. Also watch that light added to illuminate acting does not destroy the visual effects you have aimed for.

THE TECHNICAL REHEARSAL

Everyone at the technical rehearsal should know its exact purpose, which is to solve *technical* problems. You may wish to comment on:

■ scene changes, whether simple or very complicated

■ lighting cues, their timing and cueing.

■ sound effects, levels and cues

■ actors' technical problems, difficult entrances and exits, the use of unusual or mechanical properties

■ costume make-up or wig problems, quick changes, unusual additions

■ stage management tasks, cueing systems, placing of props and so on.

You will not always know exactly why the rehearsal has been stopped. Actors on stage have most difficulty; they cannot see all the problems and the attempts to solve them. You can help when asked by explaining clearly what is happening and how they can help solve the particular technical problem. Everyone has to be patient, tolerant and attentive during the technical rehearsal.

AT THE DRESS REHEARSAL

The dress rehearsal gives you your first chance to see the results of your planning and designing. You will see things to be altered and problems needing visual solutions. Make notes of all of them:

■ look for any unfinished or unconvincing painting. You may decide to brighten or tone down a colour to make it fit the picture

■ a mechanical device, a sticking door or any special effect that is not working will need attention

■ properties that do not fit or are cumbersome may need replacing or altering

■ light leaks (gaps in scenery that reveal light sources) must be blocked with a dense black material.

You will often be asked to tell actors how something is supposed to work, and you may have to change it to make things easier for them. They must perform a variety of tasks and this is a tense and difficult time for them so you must be calm and supportive.

OPENING NIGHT

A first performance is always nerve-racking, even for the designer, but the climax of all your effort will still demand work from you. You must give support to the people backstage who have to perform the show. Actors, stage hands and stage management will all greatly appreciate 'good luck' wishes and any other boost to their confidence that you can offer. You may be required to talk to sponsors, members of supporter organizations, local dignitaries, even critics. In fact you may have no time for 'first night nerves'.

TROUBLESHOOTER'S GUIDE TO FIT UPS

Tackling last-minute problems.
Technical rehearsals will reveal problems for the whole production team to solve. Some of them crop up time and again, and many have simple solutions. This chart offers suggestions for tackling recurring difficulties.

PROBLEM	SOLUTION
DOORS	**To make a door stay open.** A wooden wedge screwed to the floor will trap the under edge as it is opened. **To make a door close** A Marie Tempest device – a cord tied to a screw-eye in the top of the door passes through more screw-eyes in the top and side of the door frame. A weight on the cord is hidden behind the side of the door. Automatic opening and closing Spring hinges will keep a lightweight door closed or open. Used with nylon cord they provide automatic op ening or closing.
CANVAS	**Bulging canvas** Tighten canvas by brushing very hot water on to its reverse side. **Flapping** An extra batten can be inserted at the rear of the flat to stretch out a flap ping canvas. **Light showing through.** Paint carefully with black emulsion on the rear side.
GAPS	**Light leaks** Staple or glue opaque black cloth on the rear of adjacent flats to prevent light leaks. **Gaps in view** Glue newspaper with paint over gaps on the front of scenery.
NOISE	**Rostra** Felting (see pp.xx) should be done before the fit up. It can be applied to the underside of rostra, the tops of rostra rails or the soles of shoes if noise is discovered later. **Squeaking** Squeaks are caused by surfaces rubbing together. Try a spray lubricant or, for rostra, tighten joins with G-clamps.

SLIPPERY SURFACES	**Gradients** Generally gradients should not be steeper than 1:6 but a shiny surface on this slope will be difficult. Strips of texture, plastic compound or glued-down canvas will give grip for the feet.
REFLECTIVE SURFACES	**Mirrors** Spray with hair laquer or paint with emulsion glaze. **Floors** Dust with Fullers Earth.
PAINTING	**Too bright** Cover with emulsion glaze mixed with a small quantity of complementary colour **Paint-resistant surfaces** Add detergent to paint **Bleeding colour** If overpainting does not prevent colour bleeding paint the surface with black ernulsion paint. Re-prime in white before returning to set colour.

CHAPTER 10

STAGE PROPERTIES

Getting the right props for a production is very important. Furniture, decorative objects, household paraphernalia and the things handled by the actors will add the finishing touches to your setting. If they seem incongruous or inappropriate they will cast doubt on the accuracy of your whole design.

TO HIRE OR TO MAKE?

Having decided what you want, you have to find it. There are three ways of getting a property for your production. You can borrow it if some kind person is willing to loan it. Some people will lend things in return for a free credit or advertisement in your programme. Do not borrow a very valuable item unless you know it will be safe. Be sure that it will not be used roughly and that it can be stored safely. You may consider insuring such an item against loss or damage.

You can hire props from a shop or a specialist theatrical hirer. They have supplies of period furniture and other properties covering every aspect of daily life and you will find many suitable items. The firms charge a weekly hire fee based on the value of the item. It can be expensive to hire several pieces for a long period.

You can decide to *make* the prop for a number of reasons:

■ it may have a special use. You could, for instance, want a mechanical device built into

it, or the action may demand that the prop be thrown across the stage or climbed over

■ it may need to be a particular size to fit an actor or a difficult stage space, or the script may demand an outsize or miniature version of an ordinary item

■ if your production is to have a long run your budget may limit hiring bills

■ a setting with an individual style will seem incomplete without properties in the same fashion

■ you will use it again in subsequent productions.

A PROP-MAKER'S TOOL KIT

Basic, essential prop-makers' tools:

■ hammer
■ saws, including back saw and fret saw
■ various screwdrivers
■ pliers for bending and cutting wire
■ tin snips
■ wood chisels
■ files
■ bradawl
■ sharp craft knife
■ ssorted paint and glue brushes
■ electric drill
■ several plastic and metal buckets
■ scissors
■ sewing kit
■ drawing equipment – compasses, set squares, rulers, straight edges etc.

Below is a list of materials that you will need frequently and can keep in stock.

- timber and boards of different kinds – hardboard (Masonite), plywood, blockboard
- cane, either plastic or real
- dowelling in various thicknesses
- nails, screws, tacks, staples
- old newspaper, rags, canvas
- felt, both toymaker's thickness and heavy-weight
- wire netting, galvanized wire, fuse wire, flower-maker's wire
- tapes: brown paper, plastic, masking, 'gaffer' etc.
- emulsion paints, varnishes, French enamel varnish, spray paints, gold and silver powders.
- adhesives – latex, contact, water paste, glue size, PVA woodworking adhesive
- Modelling materials: clay, Plasticene, plaster bandage, plaster of paris etc.

WORKING DRAWINGS FOR PROPS

You must give the property makers all the information you can. They can work from photographs or pictures in a book if you find the right image but it is a poor way to present information. A book can be damaged in a workshop and a photograph is unlikely to have the right information about scale or colour.

By far the best thing to work from is a drawing. It can show several views of the prop and clearly indicate every measurement. The colours will be exactly as you want them and you can add a handy list of notes on the side. You can also add further details drawn or stuck on in the form of photocopies.

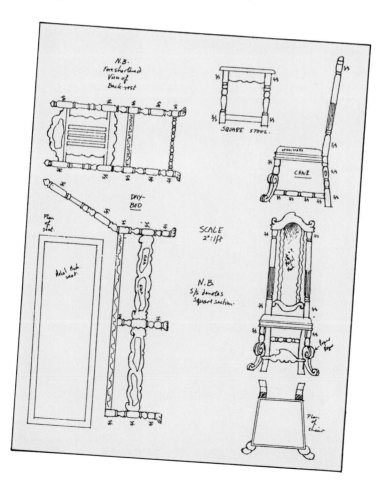

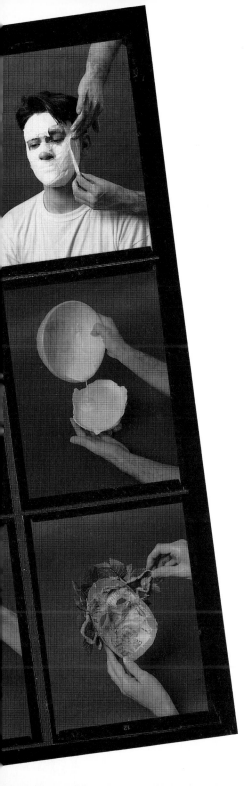

BUILDING A MASK

There are many ways of making a mask but the one shown here is particularly useful. Papier mâché is a universal prop-making medium because it is so versatile. It is always made from torn pieces of newspaper. Do not use scisssors; you need the fibrous edges to merge together and reinforce the material.

■ grease the subject's face thoroughly, especially the eyebrows and eyelashes
■ cut plaster bandage into small pieces, dip them in water and apply them to the face right up to the hairline and well under the chin. Leave the nostrils open and use several layers of plaster bandage round the edge
■ the plaster will dry very quickly. Pull it off firmly but carefully. You now have a negative mould of the face
■ hold the mask up to the light and spot the open pores in the mould. Fill these and the nostril holes on the outside with more bandage. Build it into a bowl shape by adding to the sides, especially at the chin end
■ grease the inside of the mould and pour wet plaster of paris into it. When this is dry remove the bandage and you will have a positive image of the face
■ lubricate the surface and press dry torn pieces of tissue paper to it, then build up several layers of papier mâché for the mask.
■ Pull the mask off the mould and neaten the edges and eye holes with pieces of brown paper gum-strip. Line the with lint
■ Paint and decorate the mask

A THRONE

The carpentry in the foundation of this throne is very elementary. It is the decorative techniques that make it such an impressive scenic piece. They have many applications: the paper rope, stiffened felt and assembled found-pieces can be used to elaborate furniture, armour, goblets and every kind of hand prop. Wire netting is the foundation for most three-dimensional scenic elements, such as statues, trees and rocks. The latex-dipped paper is a tough alternative to papier mâché.

■ build a simple chair base in plywood
■ using 25mm (1in) wire netting model the animal sculptures for the throne legs, squeezing it to shape and stapling it into place
■ cover the wire with paper dipped in liquid latex, taking care to marry the sculptures to the wood (papier mâché is an alternative medium)
■ decorate the sides with paper rope glued in place with a hot glue gun. The back of the throne is built up with thick felt dipped in the latex or carpenter's glue. The mouldings are produced with the same material applied in layers
■ finishing touches are added with a layer of filler – plaster or cellulose – and a foundation coat of paint. The gold effect is painted on top and supplemented with stuck-on highlights of metallic paper.

ARTIFICIAL FLOWERS

LEAVES

■ using lightweight cotton fabric prepare two or three shades of a similar green. It can be done by dying a white cloth or bleaching a coloured one

■ Cut leaf-shaped stencils in three sizes from cardboard

■ Place the stencils on the fabric, draw round them and cut out the leaves

■ Glue covered flower wire along the centre of each leaf to provide stiffness and an attachment to the stalk. A rubber-based glue or contact adhesive is best for this

■ your leaves will need no more support, but painting with a fabric stiffener will give them a crumpled effect if you want it.

A ROSE

■ cut a gradated connected petal pattern from white cotton using a cardboard stencil and also make some separate petals

■ dip the straight edge of the connected petals in latex adhesive and coil it together arranging the petals as you do so. You are forming a bud which will get looser as you move from the centre

■ glue the separate petals to the outside, pleating them as you do so to curl them back

■ add a small piece of crumpled green cloth to the underside of the completed flower for a wire to be attached

■ dip the flower into a bowl of dye while taking care to leave the base of the petals white

■ add a wire stem and leaves or attach the flowers to a real twig.

A ROMAN BREASTPLATE

The process of turning a piece of felt into a stiffened shape is useful for many prop-making jobs. Here it is used to make armour, but it can also produce vases, head-dresses or decoration on statues.

■ use a male tailor's dummy to prepare a muslin pattern for the correct shapes of the front and back pieces of the breastplate. Be sure it is adjusted to the correct size
■ transfer the pattern to heavy industrial felt – about 9mm (⅜in) thick – and cut out
■ cover the dummy with a polythene bag and pin the felt front piece to it to mould the pectoral shapes for the armour
■ prepare a dilute solution of hot glue size and dip the felt into it. Squeeze out any excess and pin the felt shape to the dummy, being sure to pin round the muscular shaping. The glued felt will dry very stiff in about 24 hours. It can then be removed and the back piece done in a similar fashion
■ add any further decoration and sew straps to shoulders and sides. Eyelets and laces are an alternative form of fastening
■ a layer of latex or several coats of paint and gold highlights will give the breastplate a finished metallic look.

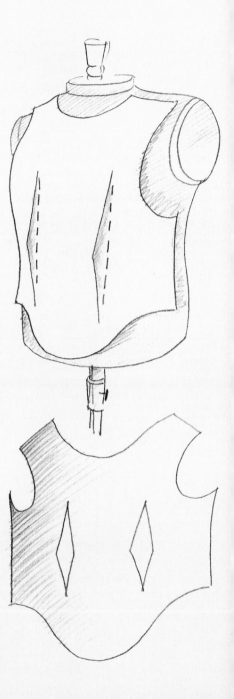

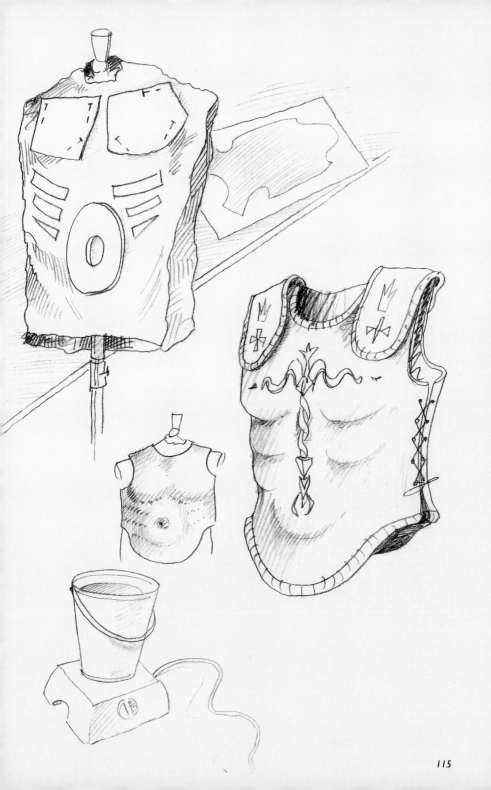

MORE PROPS
ANIMAL HEADS

Make a wire or cane frame in the shape of the head. Bind the structure together with masking tape, forming circles and making it as strong as possible. If necessary make a right-angled bend in the wire and bind that into place.

Cover the frame with pieces of fine muslin, attaching them with rubber-based glue. Now add a finishing layer of fur fabric in small pieces, a mane, eyes made of rubber-mâché and any additional detail. Leave eye-holes for the wearer and disguise them with a piece of painted sharkstooth gauze (scrim).

A CHURCH CANDLESTICK

Cut the base legs from one-inch plywood and fix them at rightangles to each other. Use plastic drainpipe for the shaft of the candlestick and fix a plastic bowl to the top with contact adhesive. Join the pieces together and decorate the feet and bosses on your candlestick with paper or hemp rope, felt shapes and nuts and washers. The plastic is a very good base for a gold paint finish.

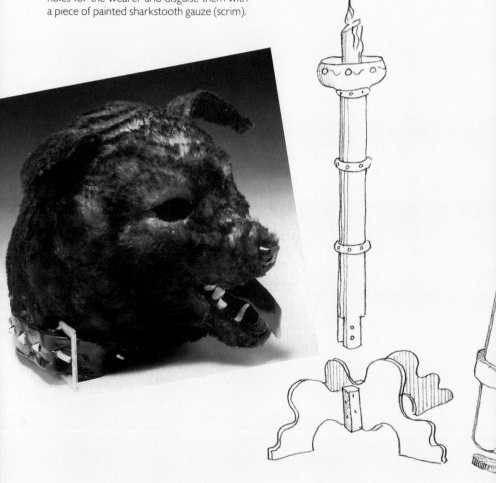

A SWORD BELT

Cut the scabbard sides out of heavy card-board and cover them with felt, using a flap to join them together. The mouth of the scabbard is kept open with a former shaped out of a block of balsa wood; a similar device shapes the bottom. Use contact adhesive to attach decorative bands of thick felt to form a belt loop.

A belt can be made from artificial leather stitched to thick felt. Glue any extra decoration into place, secure large eyelets and attach the buckle. The whole belt can be dipped in liquid latex as a preliminary coat or several coats of paint can be used to give it a metallic finish.

The sword handle can be made from carved balsa wood, taped with brown gum-strip and decorated with string patterns.

A VASE

Use a real vase as a base, greasing it and covering it with several layers of papier mâché. Cut down either side when the material is dry and remove the mould. Tape the two sides together and fix them with layers of papier mâché both inside and out.

There is no satisfactory way of making a breakable vase; the main problem is reproducing the noise of smashing ceramic, but if the sound is not an essential effect cover your paper vase with glass fibre, leaving a separate piece to be fixed in place with tape inside your pot. The easiest way of buying glass fibre is in car repair kits.

THE CROSSBOW

The shaft for this crossbow is made from two pieces of 12 mm (1/2 in) plywood, screwed and glued together. This is then cut to shape with a jigsaw and formed with a rasp. The mechanisms are made from cardboard, cut and glued into place and coated with rubber solution. The trigger is made from wire and brown adhesive tape. The actual bow consists of a strip of aluminium carpet edging, bent to the desired shape. Black emulsion paint, rubbed over-with metal polish, gives the effect of steel.

CROWNS

Make a paper pattern to ensure that your crown is the right size and shape, then cut it out of milliners' buckram. Save your paper pattern. Fix the crown into a circle and sew milliners wire *all* round the inside edges. You may need one or two wire verticals for added support.
Use your paper pattern to cut out a gold fabric or artificial leather and glue it to the outside of the crown. You can fold it over the edges for a neat finish or add gold piping and sequined effects. Jewel mounts can be built up with ironmongery or faceted candies.

GUNS

The gun barrel is made from dowel and added to a carved butt. Any details can be put on with felt, glued components or balsa wood. Triggers can be formed from wire covered with brown gum-tape.
The paint finish on your gun is very important. Gun metal can be simulated by painting the metal parts black and then overpainting a coat of shellac mixed with silver powder and black.

GOBLETS

Fix a dowel into a wooden base and attach it to a suitable plastic bowl or plant holder. Make it firm with the decoration of felt shapes at the foot and neck. String or papier mâché can also be used for decoration.

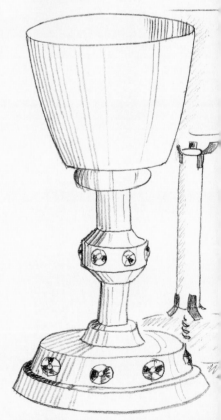

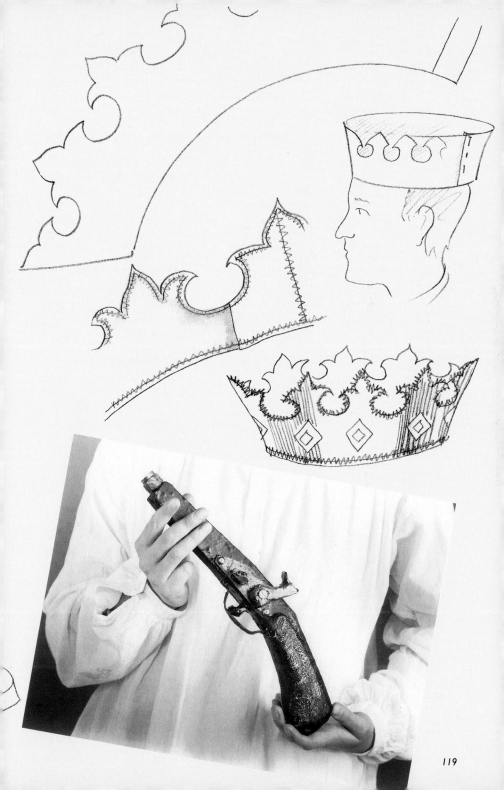

SOME COMMON PROPS

A BABY

To get weight distribution right in a prop baby, make the body out of a stuffed cloth bag and the head out of a turnip. Model a face by gluing cotton wool to the turnip, then putting it into a nylon stocking. Sew the two parts together and wrap the 'baby' in a shawl.

MEAT AND POULTRY

Chickens are best made from cotton cloth stuffed with wadding. Make the limbs separately, sew the bird together and dip it in latex. Your paint for a roast chicken should finish with a layer of brown shellac.

Joints of meat can be made with cane frames stuffed with paper and covered with papier mâché.

FOOD

Real bread will keep indefinitely if coated with a shellac or polyurethane paint. Fruit like apples and pears can be carved from polystyrene and coated in latex.

Vegetables such as cauliflowers and cabbages can be made with cloth dyed in appropriate colours, dipped in thin glue size for a crinkled effect and then sewn together.

MUSICAL INSTRUMENTS

A lute or other stringed instrument can be fashioned out of an appropriately shaped plastic bowl added to a wooden neck. Keys and other details can be made from wire covered with tape and felt.

Make trumpets out of cane frames with papier mâché covering.

Harps can be simple wooden shapes decorated and stringed .

MANACLES

Use plastic drainpipe for the cuffs and fix a chain between them with small bolts through drilled holes.

SPEARS

Cut spear blades out of soft aluminium. (A good source of this is metal lawn edging, which can be cut with old scissors and hammered into shape.) Join two sides of metal around a carved centre with clear adhesive tape. The dowel shaft and the spearhead are shaded with an FEV paint.

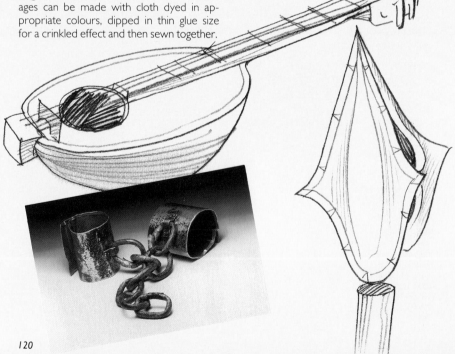

Glossary

A

Anti-pros (US) see Front-of-House lights

Apron extension of stage beyond the proscenium

ASM assistant stage manager

Auditorium area in which the audience is accommodated during the performance

B

Backcloth cloth usually painted, suspended from Flies at the rear of the stage

Backing (1) cloth or solid pieces placed behind doorways and other openings on sets to conceal stage machinery and building (2) financial support for a production

Bar horizontally flown rod (usually metal) from which scenery, lighting and other equipment are suspended

Bar bells bells sounded in all front-of-house areas to warn audience that the performance is about to continue. Operated from prompt corner, and so usually written into prompt copy

Barndoor adjustable shutters attached to stage lights to control the area of light covered by a particular lamp

Batten (1) see Bar (2) piece of wood attached to flown cloth to straighten it and keep it taut (3) piece of wood joining two flats (4) a group of stage lights suspended over the stage

Beam light a light with no lens, giving a parallel beam

Beginners call given by deputy stage manager to bring those actors who appear first in the play to the stage

Bifocal spot spotlight with additional shutters to allow hard and soft edges

Black light ultra violet light

Blocking the process of arranging moves to be made by the actor

Board lighting control panel

Book (1) alternative term for the scripts (2) the prompt copy (3) the part of a musical show conducted in dialogue

Book flat two flats hinged together on the vertical

Booking closing a book flat

Boom a vertical lighting bar

Boom arch used to hang a lantern from a boom

Border flown scenic piece designed to conceal the upper part of the stage and its machinery or equipment

Box set setting which encloses the acting area on three sides. Conventionally in imitation of a room in which the fourth wall has been removed

Brace portable support for flats

Bridge walkway above the stage used to reach stage equipment

C

Call (1) warning given at intervals to technicians and actors that they are needed on stage (2) notice of the time at which actors will be required to rehearse a particular scene

Callboard notice board on which calls and all other information relevant to the production should be posted

Cans headsets used for communication and co-ordination of technical departments during a performance

Centreline imaginary line drawn from rear to front of stage and dividing it exactly in half. Marked as CL on stage plans

Channel a circuit in the lighting or sound system

Chase a repeated sequence of changing lighting states

Check to diminish the intensity of light or sound on stage

Cinemoid a colour medium or filter

Circuit the means by which a lantern is connected to a dimmer or patch panel

Clamp C or G clamps are attached to lights to fasten them to bars

Cleat fixing on the back of flats to allow them to be laced together (cleated) with a sash line or cleat line. Also a metal fly rail to which ropes are tied

Clothscene scene played before downstage drop or tabs, while a major scene change takes place

Colour call the list of coloured gels required for a lighting design taken from the plan of the lighting design

Colour frame holder for the colour medium or filter in front of the light

Colour Medium translucent filter material placed in front of lights to give a coloured illumination

Colour wheel in lighting, a device attached to lamps which, when rotated, charges the colour medium through which the light is shown

Come down (1) instruction to actor to move towards the audience (2) instruction to lower intensity of sound or light (3) end of performance; time when curtain comes down

Corner plate triangle of plywood used to reinforce the corners of a flat

Counterweights mechanical system used for raising and lowering flown scenery

Counterweight flying the system of flying scenery, lights etc., whereby the flown item is balanced by counterweights

Crossfade the practice of moving to a new lighting or sound effect without intervening darkness or silence: one effect fades out simultaneously with the new one's being brought into play

Crossover (1) the device on a sound system that routes the sound of the correct pitch to the correct part of the loudspeaker; (2) the space behind the stage setting or below the stage through which actors can get from one side of the stage to the other without being seen by the audience

Cue (1) verbal or physical signal for an actor to enter or speak a line (2) point at which an effect is executed or business takes place

Cue light box with two lights, red and green, which warn an actor or technician to standby (red) and then do (green) whatever is required of them. Ensures greater precision when visibility or audibility is limited

Cue sheet list of particular effects executed by one department in a production

Cue-to-cue rehearsal of technical effects in a production with actors. The scene is rehearsed in sections beginning with a cue for standby, and concluding when the effect is finished

Curtain call process of actors appearing at the end of the play to receive audience applause. Formerly actors were called before the curtain by the audience

Curtain speech out of character address to the audience by a cast member or participant

Curtain up (1) time at which a play begins (2) a call given to the company to warn them the performance has begun

Cut cloth vertical scenic piece cut to reveal more scenery behind it. Most common in musicals

Cutting list list of materials required for scenery and set construction together with the correct dimensions of the pieces

Cyclorama undecorated backing to a stage, usually semi-circular and creating a sense of space and height. Often some theatres have permanent or standing cycloramas which have actually been built. The term is always abbreviated to cyc

D

Dead (1) the point at which a piece of scenery reaches the desired position onstage (2) a redundant production or scenic element

Decibel dB the measurement of volume of sound

Diffusion (colour) used like a gel but to soften and spread the beam of light rather than to colour it. Also called a frost

Dim the process of decreasing the intensity of light onstage

Dimmers the apparatus whereby lights are electrically dimmed

Dip small covered hole in stage floor with electric sockets

Dock area at side or rear of stage where scenery is stored when not in use

Downstage part of stage nearest to audience

Dress circle also known as the circle. Area of seating above the stalls and below the balcony

Dressing items used to decorate a setting

Dress parade the final check of costumes before the first dress rehearsal. The cast parade each of their costumes in order before the Director and Costume Designer so that any final alterations can be made

Drop suspended cloth flown into stage area

DSM deputy stage manager

Dutchman (US) thin piece of material used to cover the cracks between two flats

E

Elevation a working drawing usually drawn accurately and to scale, showing the side view of the set or lighting arrangement

Ellipsoidal the type of reflector used in many profile spots

Entrance (1) place on a set

through which the actor may appear (2) point in the script at which an actor appears

Exit (1) the process of leaving the stage (2) point in the script at which an actor leaves the stage

F

Fader a means of controlling the output level of a lantern (lamp) or amplifier

False proscenium construction placed behind the real theatre proscenium for decorative or practical purposes

Fit-up installation of lighting, technical equipment and scenery onstage when coming into a theatre

Flash-out system to check whether the lights are functioning properly by putting them on one at a time

Flat scenic unit comprised of wood or stretched cloth applied to a timber frame and supported so that it stands vertical to the stage door. Door flats and window flats have these openings in them. Masking flats are placed at the outer edges of the acting area to disguise areas of the stage from the public

Flies area above the stage in which scenery, lighting and other equipment are kept. If whole backdrops are to be stored then the flies should be at least twice the height of the stage opening

Floodlights also called floods. Lights which give a general fixed spread of light

Floorcloth painted canvas sheets placed on the stage floor to give a specific effect

Floor pocket (US) see dip

Flown (1) scenery or equipment which has been suspended above the stage (2) flown pieces are any scenic elements which will be made to appear or disappear from view in sight of the audience

Fly the process of bringing scenery in and out of the stage area vertically

Flying (1) the process of stocking the flies (2) special effects whereby actors are suspended by wires to create the illusion of flying

Fly floor gallery at either side of the stage from which the flies are operated

Floats see footlights

Focusing the process of fixing the exact area to be lit by each light onstage

FOH Front-of-house. Any part of the theatre in front of the proscenium arch

Follow spot light directed at actor which can follow all movements

Footlights lights set into the stage at floor level which throw strong general light into performers' faces downstage

Fourth wall imaginary wall between audience and actors which completes the naturalistic room

French brace support for scenery fixed to stage

Fresnel type of spotlight with a fresnel lens which gives an even field of light with soft edges

Frontcloth see cloth

Front-of-House lights lights hung in front of the proscenium arch

Frost see diffusion

G

Gauze painted cloth screen, opaque when lit from the front, that becomes transparent when lit from behind. Often used at front of stage to diffuse total stage picture

Gel Colour medium introduced before light to alter colour of beam

Get-in/out (US) see fit-up process of bringing scenery into or taking it out of the theatre

Ghost a beam of light which inadvertently leaks from a light and falls where it is not wanted

Gobo (1) screen introduced before a stage light to give a particular image onstage (2) cut out shape that is projected

Green room general area in which cast and crew wait during performance

Grid metal frame from which all flying equipment is suspended

Groundrow raised section of scenery usually depicting bushes rocks etc.

Grouping (US) see blocking

H

Half half hour call. Warning to company given thirty-five minutes before performance

Handprop any prop handled by an actor, such as a handbag, walking stick, umbrella

Hanging attaching flying pieces to appropriate bars

Hook clamp the device that holds a lantern onto a bar

Hot lining the method by which lanterns, bulbs and cables are checked during rigging

House (1) audience (2) in opera, the entire theatre, and by implication, the company

I

Impedance a term for the electrical resistance found in a/c circuits, thus affecting the ability of a cable to transmit sound as electrical pulses. Measured in ohms

In one (US) see clothscene

Inset a small scene set inside a larger one

Iris a device within a lantern which allows a circular beam to be altered through a range of sizes

Iron a fire proof curtain that can be dropped downstage of the tabs in case of fire. Today it is usually made of solid metal and is electrically operated

K

Kill instruction to cease use of particular effect in lighting or sound

L

Ladder a ladder-shaped frame used for hanging side lights. It cannot usually be climbed

Lamp unit of lighting equipment

Lantern see lamp

Left stage left. That part of the stage to the actor's left when he is facing toward the audience

Leg cloth suspended vertically from flies and used to mask sides of stage and small areas within it

Levels (1) indicates intensity or volume of light or sound (2) raised areas onstage used for acting

Limes jargon for follow spots and their operators

Line drawings (US) see technical drawing

Linnebach projector used for projecting a picture from a gel or glass slide onto the set. Often used to give a shadow effect

Load in/out (US) see get in/out

Lose to turn off lighting or sound, or to remove an article from the set

Luminaire international term for lighting equipment. Not restricted to theatrical lighting

M

Marking (1) in use of props or scenery, the deployment of substitutes for the real object during rehearsal (2) in singing, a

means of using the voice with reduced volume and without vocalising extremes of register (3) any account of a role in which the full powers are not being used by the performer in order to save resources

Maroon a pyrotechnic giving the effect of a loud explosion

Mark out the system of lines and objects set on a rehearsal room floor to indicate the exact position of scenery and furniture. Marking out is the process of doing this

Mask to hide or conceal unwanted areas or machinery. Also used to describe one actor obscuring another unintentionally

MD musical director

Memory memory board. An advanced type of lighting control system where the required levels are stored electronically

Mezzanine area of seating above the orchestra and below the balcony. When a theatre has only a single balcony, first several rows are frequently designated the mezzanine

Mixer sound controls desk, used to mix and adjust levels of sounds from various sources

O

Offstage any backstage area not seen by the audience. Most specifically used to indicate the areas at the actor's right and left

OP opposite prompt. Stage Right (US Stage left)

Orchestra (US) see stalls

Out flying term for up

Overture (1) the music which begins a performance (2) a call to the actors and technicians that the performance is about to begin in a musical work

P

PA system the public address or any sound amplification system

Pack a number of flats all stored together

Pan (1) movement of lighting from side to side (2) used to describe water-based stage make-up (pancakes) (3) term (now nearly obsolete) to describe theatre sound installation

Parcan type of lantern which holds a par lamp

Patch border panel a panel at which the circuits governed by individual lighting dimmers can be changed

Perch lighting position concealed behind the proscenium

Periactus a tall, prism-shaped piece of painted scenery which can be revolved to show various phases

Pipe (US) see bar

Places please (US) see beginners

Platform (US) see rostrum

Plot (1) commonly used to describe the action of a play (2) any list of cues for effects used in the play

PM production manager

Practical any object which must do onstage the same job that it would do in life, or any working apparatus e.g. a light switch or water tap (faucet)

Preset (1) used to describe any article placed in its working area before the performance commences (2) also describes a basic lighting state that the audience sees before the action begins

Projector (US) see floodlight

Prompt copy fully annotated copy of the play with all the production details from which the show is run each time it is performed

Properties props. Any item or article used by the actors in performance other than costume and scenery

Props skip basket or cupboard in which props are kept when not in use

Props table table in convenient offstage area on which all properties are left prior to performance and to which they should be returned when dead

Pros proscenium arch the arch which stands between stage and auditorium. A pros arch theatre is a conventional theatre with a proscenium arch, usually without a forestage

PS prompt side. Conventionally meaning stage left, the term now refers only to the side of the stage in which the prompt corner will be found. In the US the PS is generally stage right

Prompt corner desk and console at the side of the stage from which the stage manager runs the show

Pyrotechnics any chemical effects used onstage or in wings to create lighting or special effects

Q

Quarter back stage pre-show call given twenty minutes before curtain up (ie. fifteen minutes before beginners)

R

Rail bottom or top batten of the frame of a flat

Rake the incline of a stage floor away from the horizontal; a raked stage is higher at the upstage end than at the downstage

Readthrough early rehearsal at which the play is read without action. Usually accompanied by discussion

Reflectors the shiny surfaces in the back of lighting equipment which help intensify the beam

Rigging the means of fixing lamps to appropriate bars before lighting a production

Right stage right. That part of the stage to the actor's right when he is facing the audience

Risers the vertical part of a stage step

Rostrum a raised platform sometimes with a collapsible frame used for giving local prominence to certain areas onstage

Run (1) the number of scheduled performances of a work (2) abbreviated form of run through

Runners a pair of curtains parting at the centre and moving horizontally

S

Saturation rig an arrangement of lights in which the maximum number of spotlights is placed in every possible position

Scatter the light outside the main beam of a spot

Scrim (US) see gauze

Seque musical term indicating that one number should go immediately into the next

Set to prepare the stage for action. To set up is to get ready. To set back is to return to the beginning of a given sequence

Shutter device in front of lamp to alter shape of beam

Single purchase counterweight flying system where the cradle travels the same distance as the fly bar's travel. The counterweight frame therefore occupies the full height of the side wall of the stage

Sightlines the angles of visibility from the auditorium

SM stage manager

Snap line chalk line, chalked piece of string which when stretched tight is used for making straight lines on stage

Special piece of lighting equipment whose main function is to perform a particular effect

Spiking see marking

Spill unwanted light onstage

Spot spotlight. Light giving a small circle of light, the dimensions of which can be precisely controlled by focusing

Stagger-run runthrough at which the production is pieced together, aiming at fluency but allowing for corrective stops

Stalls floor level area of seating in the auditorium

Strike instruction to remove any redundant or unnecessary object from stage

Super non-speaking actor not specifically named in the text

Swag curtains or tabs gathered together so they do not hang straight

Switchboard board from which lights are controlled

T

Tabs theatre curtains, most usually the House curtain

Tabtrack metal track on which the tabs run allowing them to open and close

Tallescope extendable ladder on wheels used in rigging and focusing lights and for minor corrections to flown pieces

Teaser short flown border used to mask scenery or equipment

Tech technical rehearsal at which all technical effects are rehearsed in the context of the whole production

Theatre in the Round acting area with audience on all sides

Throw in lighting, the distance between a light source and the object lit

Thrust stage type of stage which projects into the auditorium so that the audience can sit on at least three sides

Tilt the vertical movement of light

Tormentor (US) see teaser

Trap hole cut in stage and concealed by floor allowing access from below. Grave traps are usually double traps creating the illusion of a grave or pit. Once a common part of all theatres traps are now becoming increasingly rare

Trapeze single short hung lighting bar

Treads the flat part of stage steps

Truck movable cradle upon which scenery is placed to facilitate its movement

U

Upstage in a proscenium or thrust stage the area furthest away from the audience

W

Wagon (US) see truck

Walk-through rehearsals at which actors go through entrances, moves and exits to make clear any changes or alterations made necessary through change of cast or venue

Warning bells (US) see Bar bells

Ways the maximum number of combinations of channels on a lighting installation

Wings the sides of the stage concealed from the audience's view

Work-out in a dance or movement rehearsal, a vigorous session to prepare the body for specific work

Workshop any non-performing backstage area of a theatre

Workshop performance a performance in which maximum effort goes towards acting and interpretation rather than sets or costumes

Musical theatre special glossary

Andante walking space

Allegro happily, lightly

Allargando getting broader

Coda last section of music, often in a different tempo or mood

Cadence the resolving chords in music

Largo broadly

Lento slowly

Maestoso majestically

Presto fast

Aria solo, usually reflective in content

Duet musical number for two singers

Trio three singers

Quartet four singers

Ensemble (1) together (2) place in which all the characters all sing together

Finale (1) the end (2) by extension, a musical sequence which ends each act, often comprising different musical material but having an overall shape

MD musical director

Band parts the individual copies required by each player in an orchestra and containing only the notes for their particular instrument.

BIBLIOGRAPHY

Listed below are a representative selection of books for each of the titles in this series.

General

In the United States the Theatre Communications Group Inc. (TCG) (355 Lexington Avenue, New York, NY 10017. Tel: 212 697 5230.) has a publications department which publishes not only plays and books but also a monthly magazine of news and features called *American Theater*. It also publishes an employment bulletin for the performing arts called Art SEARCH.

In the United Kingdom Spotlight publish annually *Contacts*, a complete guide to British Stage, TV, Screen and Radio (42 Cranbourn Street, London WC2. Tel: 01 437 7631.)

Bentley, Eric *Theory of the Modern Stage*, London, 1968; New York 1976

Brook, Peter *The Empty Space*, London and New York, 1985

Brown, John R *Drama and the Theatre*, London and New York, 1971

Hoggett, Chris *Stage and the Theatre*, London and New York, 1971

Oren Parker, W L Smith, R Harvey *Scene Design and Stage Lighting*, London and New York, 1979

Stanislawski, K *An Actor Prepares*, London, 1981; New York, 1952

Costume and Make-Up

Barton, Lucy *Historic Costume for the Stage*, Boston, 1938

Barton, Lucy *Period Patterns*, Boston, 1942

Corson, Richard *Fashions in Hair*, London, 1985

Corson, Richard *Stage Makeup*, New York, 1960

Cunnington, Phillis and Lucas, Catherine *Occupational Costume in England*, London, 1967

Directing a Play

Berry, Cicely *Voice and the Actor*, London and New York, 1974

Hagen, Uta and Frankel, Haskel *Respect for Acting*, New York, 1980

Hodgson, John and Richards, Ernest *Improvisation*, London, 1978; New York, 1979

Nicoll, A *The Development of the Theatre*, London and New York, 1966

Willett, John *The Theatre of Bertolt Brecht*, London, 1983; New York, 1968

Lighting and Sound

Bentham, Frederick *Art of Stage Lighting*, London, 1980; New York, 1968

Burris-Meyer, H and Mallory, V *Sound in the Theatre*, New York 1979

Moore, J E *Design for Good Acoustics*, London, 1961; New York, 1979

Pilbrow, Richard *Stage Lighting*, London and New York, 1979

Reid, Francis *Stage Lighting Handbook*, London, 1982; New York 1976

Stage Design and Properties

Govier, Jacquie *Create Your Own Stage Props*, London and New York, 1984

Leacroft, Richard and Helen *Theatre & Playhouse*, London, 1984

Molinari, Cesare *Theatre Through The Ages*, London and New York, 1975

Oren Parker, W L Smith, Harvey R *Scene Design and Stage Lighting*, London and New York, 1979

Stage Management and Theatre Administration

Baker, Hendrik *Stage Management and Theatre Craft*, (3rd Edition), London and New York, 1981

Crampton, Esme *A Handbook of the Theatre*, London and New York, 1980

Gruver, Bert *The Stage Manager's Handbook*, New York, 1972

Reid, Francis *The Staging Handbook*, New York, 1978

SUPPLIERS AND STOCKISTS

UNITED STATES

It is impossible to give a comprehensive list of suppliers, and stockists in the space available. Those wishing to find a specific supplier should consult

Theatre Crafts Directory (P.O. Box 630 Holmes Pennsylvania PA 19043 – 9930.)

This publication gives comprehensive listings of suppliers for costume fabric, electrical supplies, dance-wear, curtains and drapes, film equipment, and flameproofing. It even lists about 50 suppliers of feathers for theatrical costumes!

Listed below are a representative selection of stockists and suppliers.

Costume, Props, Make-Up

Norcosto Inc.
3203 North Highway 100
Minneapolis
Minn. 55422
Tel: 612 533 2791

Stagecraft Industries
1302 Northwest Kearney Street
Portland
Oregon 97208
Tel: 503 226 7351

Theater Production Services
59 4th Avenue
New York
NY 10003
Tel: 914 941 0357

Tobins Lake Studios
2650 Seven Mile Road
South Lyon
Mich. 48178
Tel: 313 229 6666

Peter Wolf Associates Inc.
3800 Parry Avenue
Dallas
Texas 75226
Tel: 214 381 8000

Lighting and Sound

American Stage Lighting
Company
1331 C North Avenue
New Rochelle, NY 10804
Tel: 914 636 5538

Electro Controls
2975 South 2nd West Street
Salt Lake City
Utah 84115
Tel: 801 487 6111

Electronics Diversified
0625 S.W. Florida Street
Portland
Oregon 97219
Tel: 503 645 5533

General Electric Company
Lamp Department
Nela Park
Cleveland
Ohio 44112
Tel: 216 266 2121

Hub Electric Inc.
940 Industrial Drive
Elmhurst, Ill. 60126
Tel: 312 530 6860

Showco
9011 Governor's Row
Dallas
Texas 75247
Tel: 214 630 1188

Stage Equipment

Gothic Color Inc.
727 Washington Street
New York, NY 10014
Tel: 212 941 0977

Peter Albrecht Corporation
325 East Chicago Street
Milwaukee, Wis. 53202
Tel: 414 272 2811

SUPPLIERS AND STOCKISTS

UNITED KINGDOM

Listed below are a representative selection of suppliers and stockists.

Costume, Props and Make-Up

Bapty and Co Ltd
703 Harrow Road
London NW10 – weapon hire
Tel: 01 969 6671

Bermans and Nathans
18 Irving Street
London WC2 – period costume
Tel: 01 839 1651

Borovick Fabrics Ltd
16 Berwick Street
London WIV 4HP – theatrical
fabrics
Tel: 01 437 2180
Tel: 01 437 5020

Bristol Old Vic Hire
Colston Hall Vaults
Bristol BS1
Tel: 0272 701 026

Brodie and Middleton
68 Drury Lane
London WC2 – dyes, canvas,
metal powders and other paints
Tel: 01 836 3289

Freed Fredk Ltd
94 St Martin's Lane
London WC2 – theatrical shoes
Tel: 01 240 0432

Laurence Corner
62 Hampstead Road
London NW1 – period hats and
other unusual clothing
Tel: 01 388 6811

Old Times Furnishing Co
135 Lower Richmond Road
London SW15 – props, furniture
hire
Tel: 01 788 3551

Lighting and Sound

Ancient Lights
8 West Carr Road
Attleborough
Norfolk NR17 1AA – lighting

DHA Lighting Ltd
7 Bishops Terrace
Kennington
London SE11 – lighting
Tel: 01 582 3600

MAC (Sound Hire)
1 Attenbury Park Road
Altringham
Cheshire
WA14 5QE

Northern Stage Services Ltd
4 Beck Grove
Woodside
Shaw
Oldham O12 8NG
Tel: 0706 849469

Rank Stand Ltd
P O Box 51
Great West Road
Brentford
Middlesex TW8 9HR – sound
Tel: 01 568 9222

Theatre Projects Services Ltd
8 Blundell Street
London N7 8BA
Tel: 01 609 2121

White Light (Electrics) Ltd
57 Filmer Road
London SW6
Tel: 01 731 3291

Stage Equipment

Furse Theatre Equipment
Traffic Street
Nottingham NG2
Tel: 0602 863 471

Northern Light
134 St Vincent Street
Glasgow G2 5JU
Tel: 041 440 1771

Rex Howard Drapes Ltd
Acton Park Industrial Estate
Eastman Road
The Vale
London W3
Tel: 01 749 5881

Theatre Flooring Ltd
Kent House
High Street
Farningham
DA4 0DT
Tel: 0322 865288

Theatre Project Services Ltd
14 Langley Street
London
WC2E 9LN
Tel: 01 240 5411

INDEX